The wolf will live with the lamb,
the leopard will lie down with the goat,
the calf and the lion and the yearling together;
and a little child shall lead them.
The cow will feed with the bear,
their young will lie down together,
and the lion will eat straw like the ox.
The infant will play near the cobra's den,
and the young child will put its hand into the viper's nest.
They will neither harm nor destroy
on all my holy mountain,
for the earth will be filled with the knowledge of the LORD
as the waters cover the sea.

—Isaiah 11:6–9 (NIV)

MYSTERIES *of* BLACKBERRY VALLEY

Where There's Smoke
The Key Question
Seeds of Suspicion
A Likely Story
Out of the Depths
Run for the Roses
Crooks and Christmas Cookies
Smoke and Mirrors
No Love Lost
The Cookbook Clue
The Final Cut
A Brush with Danger

MYSTERIES *of* BLACKBERRY VALLEY

A Brush with *Danger*

BETH ADAMS

Guideposts

A Gift from Guideposts

Thank you for your purchase! We want to express our gratitude for your support with a special gift just for you.

Dive into *Spirit Lifters*, a complimentary e-book that will fortify your faith, offering solace during challenging moments. Its 31 carefully selected scripture verses will soothe and uplift your soul.

Please use the QR code or go to **guideposts.org/ spiritlifters** to download.

Mysteries of Blackberry Valley is a trademark of Guideposts.

Published by Guideposts
100 Reserve Road, Suite E200
Danbury, CT 06810
Guideposts.org

Scripture references are from the following sources: *The Holy Bible, King James Version* (KJV). *The Holy Bible, New International Version* (NIV). Copyright © 1973, 1978, 1984, 2011 by Biblica, Inc. Used by permission of Zondervan. All rights reserved worldwide. www.zondervan.com.

Cover and interior design by Müllerhaus
Cover illustration by Bob Kayganich at Illustration Online LLC.
Typeset by Aptara, Inc.

ISBN 978-1-965859-08-7 (hardcover)
ISBN 978-1-965859-09-4 (softcover)
ISBN 978-1-965859-10-0 (epub)

Printed and bound in the United States of America
10 9 8 7 6 5 4 3 2 1

A Brush with
Danger

Chapter One

When Hannah Prentiss arrived at Bluegrass Hollow Farm, she saw that Liam Berthold's vehicle was already in the driveway. She smiled at the sight of her fiancé and his friend Archer Lestrade chatting outside the cottage with her best friend, Lacy Minyard.

Lacy waved at Hannah's car on the narrow lane. One hand rested on her round baby bump, while the other gestured at the cottage. She was upset about something—that was clear from the expression on her face. What was going on?

"Good morning," Hannah called through the open window as she parked beside Liam's Jeep. She grabbed the tray of coffees and the bag of bagels she'd picked up on the way over and hurried toward the group. Lacy's truck and a truck that must belong to contractor Gus Brody were also parked in the gravel parking area. A dumpster sat by the side of the house. The little cottage on the farm was tucked back into the woods, surrounded by beech and redbud trees, and even though its porch sagged and one of the gutters hung loose, it was a cute place. Or it would be, once the Minyards got done fixing it up.

"It's good to see you," Liam said, leaning over to kiss her cheek. She beamed as his lips brushed her skin. It had only been a few weeks since he'd proposed. Hannah had been told that she wouldn't always get butterflies when she saw the man she loved, but she was pretty sure she would. Anyone would, she thought as she took in

Liam, standing there in his T-shirt and jeans with that goofy grin on his face, as if he couldn't believe his luck.

As if he were the lucky one.

"Hi, Hannah." Lacy stepped forward and leaned in for a hug. Hannah handed the coffees and bagels to Archer, then hugged her back.

"Hi. What's going on?" Hannah asked, pulling back.

"The police are on their way," Lacy said.

"What? Why?"

Archer passed around the coffees, and Hannah took one gratefully. "The one marked *D* is for Lacy," she said. Archer nodded and held the decaf out for Lacy.

"You're always so thoughtful about my condition," Lacy said with a grateful smile. She took a sip from the cup and then gestured at the broken front window of the little cottage. "Someone broke in last night."

"Here?" Hannah felt foolish as soon as the word left her mouth. Of course here. But why would anyone break into this little cottage? There was nothing valuable inside. No one had lived there in years. Few people even knew the cottage existed, hidden in the woods a quarter mile from the main farmhouse.

"Gus brought some tools and equipment over yesterday so we could get started with demolition first thing this morning," Lacy explained. Liam had already told Hannah he and Archer volunteered to help with that process, which was why Hannah brought them breakfast. "But when we got here this morning, we found someone had smashed in the window and taken some of the tools. A power saw, a sledgehammer, and a full toolbox. They were sitting in the living room before, right inside this window."

"That's terrible." Hannah took a sip from her coffee, willing the caffeine to kick-start her brain. It was too early on a Saturday morning for puzzles. "But why? Who even knew they were there?"

"We don't know," Lacy said. "Gus is upset, obviously."

"Of course," Hannah said. "I would be too. Is he here?"

"He and Neil are both inside," Lacy said. Neil was her husband. "The rest of us are staying out of the crime scene until the police show up."

"Probably for the best," Hannah said. "But I don't understand. This cottage has been empty for how long?" The last time Hannah had been out here, in October, there was a padlock on the door. It was May now, and she doubted anyone had been here in the meantime.

"At least a dozen years," Lacy said. "No one has so much as touched the place in all that time."

"But as soon as you get ready to start renovating, someone smashes a window and steals the contractor's tools?" Hannah shook her head. "That timing is too weird."

"I know." Lacy took another sip of her coffee. "It makes no sense."

"The missing tools are valuable," Archer said. "Someone probably took them to sell."

Hannah turned her head at the sound of tires on gravel. A police car rumbled up the driveway. "Let's hope these guys can figure it out."

Deputies Alex and Jacky Holt, brother and sister, stepped out of the car. Neil came out onto the porch, followed by Gus Brody. Gus had graying brown hair and a mustache, and he wore dusty jeans and a heavy sweatshirt with work boots. He nodded a greeting to Hannah as he stepped off the porch.

"Look how cute this place is," Jacky said, walking a step ahead of her brother. Her long brown hair was tied back in its usual ponytail. "How long has this cottage been here?"

"Forty years or so," Neil said. He was hardly a short man, but he seemed small standing next to the towering Liam and Archer.

"You've had a cottage here my whole life and I never knew about it?" Jacky demanded.

"My grandparents built it when my parents got married," Lacy said. "We're fixing it up so my mom can move into it, with the baby coming and all. Or rather, we're trying to. But someone apparently had other plans." She gestured at the broken window.

"Let's take a look," Alex said.

While the deputies went inside the house, followed by Gus and the Minyards, Hannah sidled up next to Liam, who pulled her close to his side. He smelled like soap and aftershave, and she loved the feeling of his arm around her.

"I'm sorry you haven't gotten to destroy anything yet," Hannah said.

Liam and Archer would have been glad to help in any case, but they were especially excited to help demolish the old kitchen and bathroom in the cottage. Lacy and Neil were doing as much of the renovation work themselves as they could, and bringing in Liam and Archer to help smash up unneeded cabinets and walls was a win-win. They didn't have to pay for professionals to demo the place, and Liam and Archer got to break things with sledgehammers.

"Oh, it's still happening," Liam said. "Don't worry. Once Gus gets that police report so he can file an insurance claim, we're up."

"The sledgehammer was taken, wasn't it?" Hannah asked.

"We brought our own," Archer said, grinning. "What do you think we are—amateurs?"

Hannah didn't know if sledgehammers were a tool firefighters used in their jobs or whether they both just happened to own them. Maybe both.

Archer and Liam started discussing a training drill the firefighters were preparing for the following week, and Archer mentioned a cavern he wanted to explore over in Cave City. Liam asked after Brynn, Archer's fiancée, and then the deputies came back outside.

"Are there any clues as to who did this?" Liam asked as Alex walked down the steps.

"There's not a lot to go on, but we'll do our best," Jacky said.

"We dusted for fingerprints, but not much turned up," Alex said. "We'll check with the neighbors to see if anyone heard or saw anything."

"Good luck with that," Archer said, eyeing the thick trees around the cottage.

"We didn't hear or see anything, and we're the only neighbors within a mile," Neil said.

"We'll ask anyway. It's possible someone has doorbell cam footage of a car coming this way," Jacky said. "If there's a clue out there, we'll find it."

Hannah was confident Jacky was right, and she hoped they would find something. The deputies said goodbye and left.

"In the meantime, they say we can get to work," Neil said. "Since you guys brought your own tools."

Liam released Hannah, set his coffee on the hood of his Jeep, and then walked around it to open the rear door. A few minutes later, he and Archer strode toward the cottage with sledgehammers on their shoulders.

"Just the kitchen and bathroom!" Lacy called after them.

"No worries," Liam called back.

"Probably," Archer added.

"They are a little too excited about this," Lacy said.

"Of course they are," Neil said. "How often do they get permission to go into a house with a sledgehammer and break things? It's every guy's dream."

"I've got a spare hammer in my truck," Gus said, his eyes twinkling. "Do you want to join them, Neil?"

"I mean, I won't say no," Neil said. Hannah wanted to laugh. Neil owned a bookstore and adored antique maps, but he was still a boy at heart, just like the other two. A minute later, Neil disappeared inside with his own sledgehammer, and soon they heard the first crash coming from inside the house, followed by the sound of wood splintering.

"I hope that was something that was supposed to break," Lacy said with a laugh.

There was another crash, and the sound of the men cheering and laughing.

"You want to join them?" Gus asked Hannah. "I might have another sledgehammer in my truck."

"No thank you," Hannah said, holding up her hands. "I'm here for moral support."

"Suit yourself." Gus shrugged and headed toward the house. There was another smash, and then a thud, and then a couple of raised voices.

A moment later, Neil appeared in the doorway. "Lacy? You may want to come take a look at this."

Lacy and Hannah both rushed to the door. Lacy tugged a dust mask over her face, then handed another to Hannah.

The air was choked with dust, and from the doorway Hannah could see that most of the kitchen cabinets already lay in ruins on the floor. The wall behind the top cabinets in the kitchen had been opened, and the drywall lay in pieces on top of the cabinets. The drywall on the exterior wall had giant gaps in it as well. The studs were exposed, and now that she got close, Hannah could see why they had stopped.

"This stuff was hidden behind the wall," Archer said. "We thought it might be important."

Hannah leaned forward, trying to make sense of what she was seeing. "What is that?"

Something was wedged between the studs, a rectangle wrapped in brown paper. And above it was a cylinder wrapped in the same paper.

Lacy pulled out the rectangle and tore off the paper. "What in the world?" It looked like some kind of painting. It was small, less than a foot wide and tall, and it showed a lush landscape. An elaborate gold-colored frame surrounded it.

Liam unrolled the second paper and found a canvas showing a bunch of animals and people standing around together. It looked as if it had been roughly cut from its frame.

"Lacy," Hannah said, "why are there paintings hidden in the wall of your cottage?"

Lacy shook her head. "Your guess is as good as mine."

Chapter Two

※

Lacy carried the framed picture and the canvas tube toward the wooden table in the cottage's kitchen, along with the sheets of brown paper.

Hannah found a rag to wipe off the table, and Lacy set the pieces gently on the clean surface.

"What's this?" Gus reached into the crumpled paper and pulled out a lined index card. *Cole* was written on it in spidery blue script.

"Hey, there's one in this one too," Liam said, and took another index card from the other piece of crumpled paper. *Hicks.*

"Are those names?" Lacy asked.

No one could answer her, so they all took in the framed picture. It showed a landscape, a sweeping vista from high on a mountain, with a valley traced by a river below. The top half of the painting was taken up by clouds, dark and brooding on the left side with streaks that seemed to indicate rain, giving way to white, fluffy cumulus clouds on the right side. Despite its small size, the image managed to convey a grand scale. The whole picture was tinged in a golden light and captured the vastness of the hilly landscape.

"That's pretty," Hannah said. "It doesn't look like Kentucky, does it?"

"It could be the eastern part of the state," Archer said, and Hannah realized he was right. There were hills like this over in the

Appalachian region of the state. She supposed it could be anywhere, really.

"Let's spread this one out." Lacy gently pressed down the edges of the painting that had been rolled up. This one showed a bunch of different animals, and a person in flowing robes with his arm around the neck of what looked like a tiger. A woman and small child sat nearby, and behind them all was a river and a blue sky with fluffy clouds.

"Why are there so many animals together?" Archer asked. "That lion would totally eat that cow, not sit there smiling at it."

"And the sheep there would be running for its life from that cheetah," Liam added. "It could be Noah's ark, except the numbers are wrong. There would have to be two of each animal for that."

Hannah also spotted a fox, a couple of goats, and what looked like a badger or racoon in the group of animals. None of those animals typically hung out together.

"Wait," Neil said, leaning forward. "I've seen a painting like this before. Or a picture of it anyway. It's about that Bible verse, the one that says the lion will lie down with the lamb."

"From Isaiah?" Liam asked. "'The wolf will live with the lamb, the leopard will lie down with the goat, the calf and the lion and the yearling together; and a little child will lead them.'"

"That's the one," Neil said. "I know I've seen this painting before, or at least one like it."

"Maybe it's a copy of a famous painting?" Lacy said.

Hannah noticed something on the curled-up edge of the canvas. Something was written on the back. "Edward Hicks," Hannah said when she made out the words. "I guess that *was* the artist's name on the card."

"Is Edward Hicks the guy who did the painting you were thinking of?" Lacy asked Neil.

Neil shrugged. "I honestly have no idea. I know I've seen a painting like this somewhere, but I don't remember where or who the artist was."

"I have a friend in California who might know," Hannah said. "I met Margot at Bible study. She works at the Getty Museum in LA. I could give her a call. She would probably know if Edward Hicks is an artist we should have heard of."

"Go for it," Lacy said. "I have no clue what to make of this, so I'd appreciate any information she can give."

"See if she can tell us what these paintings are doing in the wall of our cottage while you're at it," Neil added, smiling.

"Hang on." Hannah pulled up Margot's number in her phone and called her. Hopefully it wasn't too early in California. Then again, Margot had always been an early riser.

She was in luck. "Hi, Hannah," Margot said brightly. "How are you?"

"I'm great. And you?" Hannah felt awkward having the conversation with everyone standing around her, so she put the phone on speaker so they could all hear.

"Walking on the beach, enjoying the warm sunshine. You know, another day in paradise. Don't pretend you don't miss the weather here."

Hannah laughed. "I don't know. After a while, you get tired of endless sunshine and no humidity." Margot Diaz, like many of Hannah's friends back in Los Angeles, had struggled to understand why Hannah had given it all up and moved home to Kentucky. "Besides, May is beautiful here. It's warm but not too hot, and everything is in bloom. This is the real paradise."

"If you say so. How's your hunky fireman?"

Liam grinned, while Gus and Archer snickered.

Hannah felt heat rising into her face. "He's right here. And now would probably be a good time to let you know you're on speaker."

"In that case, hi, Liam. Hannah turns into a giggling mess whenever she talks about you, so I know she's got it bad."

"Margot!" Hannah protested.

"What? It's true. Hey, Liam, do you have any single friends?" Margot asked.

"You come out for a visit, and I'll introduce you to some guys I know," Liam said, laughing.

"I've got a brother," Archer called.

"*Anyway,*" Hannah said, trying to regain control of the conversation. "I'm sorry to bother you so early, but something strange has happened. I wondered if you might be able to tell me about an artist named Edward Hicks."

"The *Peaceable Kingdom* guy? I haven't thought of him in a while. How did he come up?"

Hannah quickly recounted the story of how they'd uncovered the two paintings.

"They're prints?" Margot clarified.

Hannah leaned forward and studied the surface of the paintings. "No, they're paintings. If you look closely, you can see the brushstrokes."

"Can you send me a picture?"

Hannah snapped a photo of each and texted them to her.

"Got them. The first one looks like one of Edward Hicks's *Peaceable Kingdom* paintings," Margot said. "Or a copy of it, anyway. And the other one looks like the work of someone from the Hudson River School. Durand, or Church, or maybe Cole— someone in that vein."

Hannah didn't know the names Margot was reeling off, and judging by the faces around her, she guessed the others in the room didn't either.

"There was a card with it that said Cole."

"Thomas Cole then. From the Hudson River School, an informal group of artists whose paintings celebrated nature. They painted landscapes, mostly in the Romantic style, and they generally showed big, expansive views and sweeping vistas like this one. They had a big influence on nineteenth-century American art. Edward Hicks was a Quaker minister who made a series of paintings called *Peaceable Kingdom*, based on that verse in Isaiah. The lion shall lie down with the lamb—you know the one. He made sixty-something paintings in this series, and each is a little different, but they all represent the same subject matter. My guess is they're probably copies, but they're really pretty. What a cool find."

"Maybe we can hang them in the cottage once we get it renovated," Lacy said.

"I like that idea if your mom is on board," Neil said.

"Hang on," Margot said. "I put the image you sent me into a web image search, and—this is odd."

Margot stopped, and Hannah held her breath. She looked around the room and saw that everyone else was looking at the phone, waiting to hear what Margot said next.

"*Where* exactly did you say you found these paintings?" Margot finally asked.

"Buried behind some drywall in a cottage on my friend Lacy's farm," Hannah said. "Why?"

Margot didn't say anything for a moment, and Hannah tried to be patient, but she felt her heartbeat speed up.

"Hannah, I put those pictures into an image search and they both turned up."

"If they're copies of paintings by famous artists, that makes sense," Hannah said. There would likely be images of the original paintings on the internet.

"No—I mean, yes, it would make sense, but it's *why* they turned up that's odd. Hannah, the originals of these paintings were both stolen from a museum in Kentucky in 1990. An Edward Hicks *Peaceable Kingdom* painting and a small Thomas Cole landscape in a gold frame were among the paintings that went missing from the Witherspoon Museum in Frankfort, Kentucky, in one of the biggest art heists of all time. They were stolen, and they haven't been seen since."

"What?" Hannah couldn't come up with anything more intelligent to say.

"You haven't heard of this? It's a big deal. It was one of the most brazen art heists ever carried out. There was even a true crime podcast about it a couple years ago. Two guys tied up the night security guard and stole several artworks from the museum. Only one piece has turned up over the years, but the rest were never recovered."

"Is there any chance these paintings are originals?" Lacy said. "Like, the ones from the museum?"

"I don't know," Margot said. "But if they are original paintings, they're worth *a lot*, and they've been stolen. You have to call the police."

Chapter Three

Jacky Holt shook her head as she stepped out of the police car. "You guys couldn't wait until we had coffee before you found something else to report stolen?"

"I think you'll want to see this," Neil said, and the somber tone of his voice seemed to signal to Jacky that the situation was not a joke. She nodded and followed everyone inside, with Alex on her heels. Neil explained how they'd opened the wall and found the paintings wedged between the studs, and then Hannah told the officers what they'd learned from Margot.

"You're saying these pictures were stolen from an art museum?" Alex asked, staring at the Thomas Cole painting.

"We're not sure they're genuine," Hannah said. "But if you look up the theft at the Witherspoon Museum in Frankfort, you'll see that they're listed as two of the paintings that were never recovered." Hannah had done a quick search while they waited for the police to arrive, and now showed the officers the results on her phone.

"It would be a pretty strange coincidence if copies of two of the stolen paintings were found together like this," Jacky said. "And with visible brushstrokes and artist signatures. And here's a picture of the landscape one at the museum—in a frame identical to this one. I think we have to assume these are the real deal. We have to call Sheriff Steele."

"And we'll need everybody to wait outside for now," Alex added. "Once the sheriff has taken a look around, we may be able to let you back in, but for now, this is a crime scene."

Hannah, Lacy, Archer, Liam, Neil, and Gus all shuffled out and stood in the shade of a redbud tree while the police officers investigated inside the cottage.

"So, let's say those really are paintings that were stolen from an art museum," Archer said. "How did they end up here?"

"I don't have any clue," Lacy said, taking off her dust mask. "It doesn't make any sense."

"Here's an article about the theft," Liam said, looking at his phone. "From the *Frankfort State Journal*. THIRTY YEARS LATER, STILL NO CLUES ABOUT ARTWORK STOLEN FROM WITHERSPOON MUSEUM. It's from several years ago."

"What does it say?" Lacy asked.

"It says ten pieces of priceless and important American art were stolen from the Witherspoon Museum in Frankfort, and that only one piece—an abstract work by Mark Rothko—has been recovered. Let's see." Liam read a bit more and then continued summarizing. "The Witherspoon Museum is a private collection in Frankfort. It was originally owned by the Witherspoon family and turned into a museum in 1977, and it held what was generally considered to be one of the finest collections of American art at the time of the theft. In the thirty years since the theft, several law enforcement agencies, including the FBI and Kentucky State Troopers, have investigated, but no luck."

"Wow," Lacy said. "That's so sad."

"The theft was apparently one of the boldest museum heists of all time. It says, 'On the night of February 24, 1990, two men wearing ski masks approached the side entrance of the museum. They were admitted by the night guard, who was in his early twenties and had only been employed by the museum for two months at the time. Against protocol, the guard let the men inside, where they promptly tied him up and blindfolded him. Authorities have long questioned why the guard let the men inside and whether he might have been involved with the theft itself, but have never been able to connect him to the break-in directly.'"

"That does sound suspicious," Hannah said.

"It also says that security cameras inside the museum captured footage of the thieves walking into the galleries and taking the most important and valuable works. They stuffed the paintings into large canvas bags, and in some cases removed large canvases from the frames with knives and rolled them up before stuffing them into bags. Then they left, leaving the guard tied up, and he was stuck there until the day guard showed up for his shift."

"Yikes," Neil said. "That's awful."

"The stolen items included paintings by Andy Warhol, Georgia O'Keefe, and several other well-known artists," Liam said, continuing to summarize. "The director of the museum is quoted as saying the thieves knew what they were doing because they took only the most valuable pieces. And it asks for anyone with information about the theft to come forward."

"That's crazy," Lacy said. "But the question for us is how did two of the paintings come to be here of all places? In a little private cottage on a farm in Blackberry Valley. It doesn't make any sense."

They all looked up at the sound of tires on gravel, and a moment later, the sheriff's sedan parked on the dirt driveway. Sheriff Colin Steele was in his forties, with salt-and-pepper hair and a thin, wiry frame. He was well-respected in the community, but Hannah wondered if he'd ever encountered a crime on this scale.

"I'm told you've had some excitement this morning," Colin said. "Between stolen tools and stolen paintings, this renovation is turning out to be a doozy."

In all the excitement over the paintings, Hannah had almost forgotten about the break-in and the missing tools.

"We like to keep our sheriff's department limber," Neil said. "Thank you for coming. I hope you didn't have any trouble finding the place."

"Not at all," Colin said. He gazed at the cottage for a moment. "It's been a while, but I've been here before."

"You have?" Lacy said.

Colin nodded, but didn't elaborate before he started for the door. "If this is what we think it is, you're probably done with demolition for the day. We're going to need to keep things as they are while we look into what happened."

Hannah sensed disappointment settling over the rest of the group. Liam and Archer were no doubt sad they wouldn't get to smash more things, but for Lacy, it was different. The clock was ticking to get this renovation done so her mom could move in before the baby came, so the delay was frustrating.

"Why don't you all head home?" Neil suggested. "I'll stick around to answer any questions the police have and lock up. There's no sense in everyone hanging out here all day."

"I guess that works," Archer said. He sounded resigned.

"And I'll let you guys know once they give the all-clear to start smashing things again," Neil added. "You can come back and finish the job."

That cheered Archer up. "I'll see you at the station later?" he asked Liam.

"I'm actually not working today," Liam said. "My parents are coming to visit, remember? Hannah and I are taking them out to dinner tonight."

Hannah's stomach churned at the words. She was excited to finally meet Liam's parents, who had come to town to celebrate his mother's sixty-fifth birthday. And, she suspected, to meet their son's fiancée. She was glad they were coming from Florida to visit, but she was also nervous. She wanted to make a good impression.

"That's right," Archer said. "I forgot. Have fun with them."

"We will," Liam said. "And maybe this delay is good after all. It gives me time to go home and clean up before they arrive."

"Well, I know where I'm going," Lacy said. "I'm headed straight over to ask my mom whether she knew about those paintings. She lived on the farm, after all, so maybe she knew they were there."

"You should definitely talk to your mom," Hannah said. "But if she knew the paintings were there, why wouldn't she have reported them? I can't believe she could have known about the stolen paintings and not said anything."

"She knew we were going to demo the kitchen," Neil added. "We're lucky Liam spotted them before a sledgehammer went through one of them. Even if your mom had somehow known about the stolen paintings being on the property all this time—which, like

Hannah said, I highly doubt—she wouldn't have let us risk destroying them or damaging them, not if they are these priceless pieces."

"You're right," Lacy said reluctantly. "I mean, of course you're right. Mom would never keep something like this a secret. But I still want to talk to her, if only to learn more about the history of the cottage. *Someone* had to know those paintings were there. Maybe she can tell us who had access to the cottage all these years. Hannah, do you want to come?"

Hannah had chores to finish and some invoices to process before heading in to the restaurant for a bit. She probably should spend some time getting herself ready to meet Liam's parents for the first time.

But she couldn't deny that she was curious about what Lacy's mom had to say.

"I don't know why you're hesitating," Lacy said. "I know you want to come with me and find out if my mom has any clues to this mystery."

"You know me too well," Hannah said with a chuckle. "All right. I'll meet you at your mom's place."

Chapter Four

Hannah bumped down the rutted dirt road in her Subaru Outback, heading toward town. Once she was back on the main road, she turned on the radio and sang along as she passed farms and wound around hills until she reached the little town of Blackberry Valley. On this sunny May Saturday morning, the streets were crowded with people strolling along Main Street, window-shopping and talking in spite of the rising temperature and humidity. The dogwood and redbud trees that lined the sidewalks were full with fresh green leaves, and the flowers in the planters were in full bloom.

Hannah parked in a spot outside Jump Start Coffee. Lacy's mom, Christine, currently lived in a quaint apartment over the stationery store, a block away. Lacy had parked down the block and was waiting for Hannah on the sidewalk.

"Do you think your mom will be home?" Hannah asked as she walked up.

"I called her on the way over. She was getting ready to go grocery shopping, but she was intrigued by my questions about the cottage, so she's waiting for us."

"Oh good."

Lacy started toward her mother's door, but Hannah hesitated. "Should we bring her something? Maybe coffee, or a doughnut or muffin or something?"

"Now you're just being mean, tempting a pregnant woman with doughnuts."

Hannah laughed. "I'll take that as a yes?"

"You're right, it would be better manners to show up with doughnuts in hand," Lacy said. "Mom likes doughnuts."

"Everyone likes doughnuts."

They crossed the street and walked into Sweet Caroline's Bakery, which smelled like cinnamon and sugar. Hannah was tempted by the doughnuts but settled on a peaches-and-cream scone, while Lacy picked up a chocolate glazed doughnut for herself and an assortment for Christine to choose from, "Just in case."

"In case of what?" Hannah asked. "In case you want a second doughnut?"

"Don't judge me. I'm staring down a summer of being hot and miserable and having to run to the bathroom every five minutes. I deserve a second doughnut."

Hannah laughed and paid for the goodies, and then she carried the pink box down the street and up the stairs to Christine's apartment.

"Hello," Lacy's mom said, ushering them inside. "Good to see you, Hannah. Congrats again on the engagement. When is the big day?"

"We haven't had a chance to start planning yet," Hannah said. "But hopefully soon."

"Well, you better get on that. If I was dating Liam, I'd lock it down as soon as possible."

"Mom, Liam loves Hannah." Lacy was shaking her head. "They'll be fine."

Christine ignored Lacy's protests and pulled her in for a hug. "How are you, Lacy?"

"Hot," Lacy said as she flopped into what had been her father's recliner. Christine had moved into this apartment when her husband, Frank, passed and Lacy and Neil took over Bluegrass Hollow Farm. She'd brought much of the furniture from the farm with her.

"How about some ice water?" she asked her daughter now.

"Ice water would be great," Lacy said. "And a doughnut."

Hannah handed her the chocolate glazed, and Christine carried over a stack of small plates and a glass of ice water. Hannah declined the offer of water or coffee, but she accepted a small plate for her scone and settled on the couch, while Christine chose a glazed doughnut and took the other recliner.

"You're going to get some new furniture when you move into the cottage, right, Mom?" Lacy asked, taking a bite of her doughnut. Shards of chocolate spilled onto her plate.

"I wasn't planning on it," Christine said. "This furniture still works fine."

"Yeah, but it's so old," Lacy said. "Don't you want something new and fresh, for your fresh start?"

"I don't know," Christine said. "There's something comforting about the familiar too. It almost belongs on the farm, doesn't it?"

Hannah leaned against the couch, which she and Lacy had lounged on so many times as teenagers, and couldn't disagree. Even though the furniture was no longer in the old farmhouse, it still felt a little bit like her home away from home. But she knew better than to get in the middle of this discussion between mother and daughter, so she kept her thoughts to herself.

"Well, if you decide to get new stuff, let me know, and I'll help you pick it out," Lacy said.

Christine nodded. "I don't know. It sounds like there has been a delay in the renovation. What exactly did you find in that wall?"

Lacy recounted the story of discovering the paintings during the demolition, and what they'd learned of the heist at the Witherspoon Museum, and Christine stared until she finished. "I remember when that theft happened. It was all over the news, and—" She broke off suddenly, and Hannah waited. Christine pressed her lips together, and her gaze settled on the other side of the room for a moment, then she waved her hand and continued. "Well, anyway, it was a big deal."

What was that about?

"Mom?" Lacy asked, clearly wondering too.

But Christine was already talking again. "The theft was, what, in the early nineties or something?"

"In 1990, I think." Hannah took out her phone to double check. "Yes, it says here it happened in February of 1990."

"Well, the cottage was built in 1986," Christine said. "When Frank and I got married. So the paintings obviously weren't there when the house was built, and they weren't put there while we lived in it. We moved out of the cottage and into the main house in January 1990, after Frank's father passed. I was still pregnant with you"—she nodded at Lacy—"but we were already glad to have more space. Babies need so much gear. We rented out the cottage after we moved, so it must have happened at some point while someone else was living there. But for sure Frank didn't know, and obviously I didn't either."

"So a renter must have been responsible?" Hannah asked.

"I guess so," Christine said. "All I know is that Frank definitely didn't know about it."

The way she repeated that Frank didn't know—so quickly and so definitively—struck Hannah as just a little bit off. She glanced at Lacy to see if she noticed it too, but Lacy was already asking, "So who else lived there, and when?"

"Well," Christine said slowly. "Let's see. My friend Joanie stayed for a few weeks."

"Who?" Lacy sounded confused.

"An old childhood friend. But she didn't officially live here. She only needed a place to stay for a bit. There were several of those through the years."

"Any chance she brought the paintings?"

"No way." Christine laughed. "Not a chance. Let's see. If we're looking at long-term tenants, the first one was George. He lived at the cottage for maybe six months."

"Who's he?" Lacy asked.

"You were just a tiny thing, so I would have been surprised if you remembered him. George Fowler. He was looking to downsize after his wife passed. He was quiet, kept mostly to himself. He moved out after a fall, when he had to move into a facility that provided more care."

"Could he have known anything about the paintings?"

"I don't know," Christine said. "Even if he did, he passed many years ago, so unfortunately he's not around to ask."

"Did he have any connections to art? Or to the museum? Or..." Hannah wasn't even sure what she was asking. "Thieves?"

"He was a retired train engineer. I didn't get the sense he knew or cared much about art, but I'll be honest that I was pretty out of it in those days. Trying to keep up with a farm and a baby was hard enough, plus my dad's health was starting to fail, so it's possible he could have been an art aficionado and I would have had no idea."

"Maybe we can do some research into him," Lacy suggested to Hannah, who nodded. "Who else?"

"After George moved out, a young couple stayed there for a year or so. What were their names? She liked bugs, and he was the one who put the vegetable garden in the yard. That's long gone now, of course, but it was nice for a while. I'll have to dig around and see if I can find their names. I don't know if they had any connection to art or anything like that. And, of course, Colin and Geraldine."

"Colin and Geraldine?" Lacy asked.

"You mean the Steeles?" Hannah asked. The sheriff had lived in the cottage? Was that what his cryptic comment earlier meant?

"Yes, the sheriff and his wife lived in the cottage when they were first married back in, oh, probably 2006 or so?"

"They did?" Lacy asked. "I guess that's why he said he'd been there before."

"That would explain it," Christine said. "He has very definitely been there before. Every day for eighteen months or so. He was just starting out on the force then." She took a bite, and a few crumbs rained down onto her plate. "I never totally understood it, because with Geraldine's family, they could have afforded something much nicer, but I think they were trying to make it on their own. Trying to prove to her family that he could provide for her or something like that."

"What?" Hannah was confused. "What do you mean, 'with her family'?"

"Why, Geraldine comes from money. You didn't know that?" Christine pressed her finger against her plate to pick up the crumbs and popped them into her mouth.

"I guess I never really thought about it," Hannah said. She didn't know Geraldine very well, but the sheriff's wife always appeared polished and put together, and she dressed well. And now that Hannah thought of it, the diamond ring on her finger was larger than most around these parts. She was an artist and sold paintings from a gallery on their property.

"Like, are we talking a lot of money?" Lacy added.

"I don't know how much, really, but I think her family owns a lot of real estate in Frankfort, and I got the impression her father was in banking or something like that. I thought I heard that her family collects art, actually. Where did I hear that?" Christine thought for a moment, and then shrugged. "I don't know. Somewhere. But really, you didn't think they could afford that nice house on a sheriff's salary alone, did you?"

Sheriff Steele and his wife lived in a beautiful old Victorian house surrounded by acres of land on the outskirts of town. They had horses that Hannah always admired as she drove past. It was one of the nicest houses in the area, quite large, and on sizable acreage. All that land and those horses had to be worth a pretty penny.

"I never really thought about it," Lacy said. "Do sheriffs not make a lot?"

"Not enough to keep up with a place like that," Christine said. "Anyway, they did live in the cottage for a while."

"That's very interesting," Hannah said. She had been to Geraldine's studio once, years before, when Mom was looking for a picture to hang on the living room wall. She made mostly landscapes of the local area, and they were beautiful, and Mom had bought a painting of the sun setting over the hills.

"I don't see how they could have had anything to do with it, though," Christine said. "Given that he's a sheriff, and they lived there about fifteen years after the theft."

Hannah couldn't either, but she wrote their names down anyway, since they were making a list of people who lived in the cottage.

"Right. Who else?" Lacy asked.

"That's pretty much it for actual tenants."

"What about people who came and stayed for a short time? You said there were some of those as well."

"Like I said, Joanie. I'd need to think of who else. Honestly, by the time the Steeles moved out, the house needed some repairs and updates that were pretty expensive, like a new water heater and an upgrade to the electrical system, and there was never really enough money to make those happen, so it was hard to rent it out."

"Yeah, we recently learned about all the updates the house needs," Lacy said wryly.

"I appreciate how much you all are doing to make my new home welcoming," Christine said. This seemed to mollify Lacy, who gave her a bright smile.

"Okay, so our suspects are a retired train engineer who passed away a long time ago, an unnamed couple who planted a vegetable garden, your childhood friend, and the sheriff who is currently investigating the mystery?" Lacy said, eyebrow raised.

"Oh, I thought of another pair of short-term residents. Gordon and Elyse lived there for a while," Christine said, nodding at Hannah.

"My aunt and uncle?"

"Sure. They had a kitchen fire at their house, and they needed a place to stay while their home was being repaired, so they rented the cottage for a few months."

"I'd forgotten about that." Hannah had been at college in California when the fire happened, and though she'd heard of it from her parents, she hadn't known where the family had lived while their house was being repaired. "Ryder started it, right? Trying to deep fry candy bars or something?"

Hannah's cousin Ryder was a few years younger than she was, and he'd always had something of a wild streak, though these days he was a sedate actuary who wore button-downs and slacks to work each day. He offset that with adventures like caving, and Uncle Gordon often bemoaned his son's lack of wife and children, wondering when he'd settle down. Knowing Ryder, Hannah doubted that would happen in the near future.

Christine laughed. "I don't think I ever heard what happened. They certainly didn't go around blaming your cousin for the fire. I only know that they needed a place to stay, and so they moved into the cottage for a while."

Lacy turned to Hannah. "Do you think your aunt or uncle—"

"No way," Hannah said, shaking her head. "Not a chance. If they knew anything about those paintings, they would have said so."

"What about Ryder? Or Maeve?" Lacy asked, mentioning Ryder's older sister.

"I don't think even Ryder would have hidden stolen paintings," Hannah said. "Besides, if they had torn open the walls of the kitchen while they lived there, wouldn't you have noticed?"

"We never went in there when other people were renting the place. It was their home while they lived there. Someone could have torn out all the walls, and we wouldn't have known until they moved out." Christine seemed to consider. "But actually, I remember there was a leak in one of the pipes in the kitchen while they lived there, and if I remember right, I think Gordon did open up the wall to fix it."

"He did?" Lacy looked at Hannah, her eyes wide.

"I don't remember much more than that. I wish Frank were here. He handled so much of the stuff with the cottage. He would remember better than I do. But I'm pretty sure that happened, although I don't remember particulars. I just know that Gordon offered to fix it because he's a plumber, and we were grateful to let him handle it. I'm sure Frank must have checked on the work afterward, but I don't know."

"So you're saying that while Gordon and Elyse were living in the cottage, they opened up the walls in the kitchen?" Lacy said.

"It might not have been the part of the wall where the paintings were found," Christine said. "But yes."

"Right," Hannah said. "If he'd opened up the wall where the paintings were, he would have reported it to the police."

"Anyone else come to mind, Mom?" Lacy asked.

"Like I said, there were lots of people who needed a place to stay for a few weeks or months, for whatever reason. I'll have to try to come up with a list," Christine said.

"I can't believe we're really talking about this," Lacy said. "Who would have ever thought that something like valuable paintings could have been hidden in the cottage? It's crazy."

"Let's hope the sheriff figures it out," Hannah said.

"And soon, so we can get back to renovations," Christine added.

"In the meantime, we need to look into this ourselves, obviously," Lacy said.

Hannah wrinkled her nose. "I'm not so sure that's a good idea."

Lacy lifted her chin. "Look, I will admit I have a vested interest in this. I want to get that cottage renovated before this baby comes, and we don't have a lot of time. If the police spend weeks looking into this, who knows when they're going to let us get back in there and get to work? So, yes, obviously I'm hoping we can help speed things along."

"I also want to get this settled quickly," Christine said. "Not just because I want to move in before the baby comes, although I am a *teensy* bit excited about that—"

"Yeah, I saw your social media post where you announced that we were renovating the cottage so you could move in. I've never seen so many emojis in one post in my life," Lacy said with a chuckle.

"What? I'm excited. I'm not going to pretend otherwise. But like I said, that's not the only reason I want to get this figured out. People will think Frank had something to do with it, and he absolutely did not. So the sooner we find out who really did, the better."

Again, Hannah wondered at the vehemence with which she insisted Frank was innocent. Of course he was, so why was Christine working so hard to make sure Hannah knew that? Was it a little too much?

On the one hand, Hannah wasn't sure she wanted to get involved in something like this, with such a high-profile theft and paintings worth thousands or even millions of dollars. She didn't want to get in the way of the police investigation and potentially compromise a case this big.

On the other hand, though, she could see that Lacy was right. And she *was* curious about what had happened. Suddenly she realized she was speaking, even before she'd consciously made a decision.

"All right," she found herself saying. "We have to stay out of the way of the police. But sure, let's see what we can find out."

Chapter Five

As they went down the stairs from Christine's place, Lacy asked, "So, what are you up to now?"

"I was thinking I would head home," Hannah said. "I have a lot of things I need to take care of before meeting Liam's parents tonight."

"Like what?" The wooden stairs groaned beneath them as they made their way down.

"I was thinking I would deep-condition my hair. I need to take the chipped polish off my toenails and repaint them. I was going to iron my outfits for dinner and church tomorrow. I need to pop into work and do a few things, since I won't be working tonight. I need to clean my apartment." They reached the ground floor and started for the door.

Lacy raised an eyebrow at her. "Do you really think Liam's parents are going to see your apartment? Or your toes?"

"I hope not," Hannah said. They stepped out into the warm May sunshine and moved to the edge of the sidewalk to let the people strolling along Main Street pass. "But I want to be ready just in case. I mean, what if I want to wear open-toed shoes to church tomorrow? It's warm enough for that now. I don't want my future in-laws to think I'm a slob or anything."

"Poor foot hygiene *is* a leading cause of divorce," Lacy said, her tone so serious that it took Hannah a second to realize she was kidding.

Hannah elbowed her. "I want to make a good impression."

"Of course you do. It makes sense. You're marrying their son, becoming a part of their family. But they're going to love you, and for reasons that have nothing to do with your toes. If I'm honest, your toes are not your best feature."

"Are toes *anyone's* best feature?"

"I guess not, but some people have better-looking feet than others."

"I don't really know what you're getting at, but it's starting to freak me out. What's wrong with my feet?"

"Nothing is wrong with your feet. My point is that you don't have to stress about making a good impression. They're going to love you."

"I hope you're right."

"I'm always right." Lacy patted her arm. "Trust me, you have no reason to worry. Which is why I think you should skip cleaning and conditioning and come with me to the library."

"The library? Why?"

"For one, it's air-conditioned."

"It's not even that hot out."

"You try walking around with a bowling ball strapped to your belly, and then you can tell me if you're hot," Lacy said. Hannah supposed she couldn't argue with that. "Besides, I want to find out more about the theft itself, and I bet we can find old newspaper articles there."

"You're right, of course." Normally Hannah would be all over this plan. She did want to find out more about the art heist, and Lacy was right that the library was the logical place to do so. But she really did need to get ready, and she had to be at the restaurant in a couple of hours.

"How about this? I'll buy you a sandwich, and then we go for an hour and see what we can find out. After that, you can go home and fix your toes."

"You're trying to buy me off with a sandwich?"

"You better believe it." Lacy grinned. "Any kind of sandwich you want."

"Are you sure you're not just hungry?"

"Of course I'm hungry," Lacy said. "I'm always hungry. But that's not why I'm offering." A moment later, she added, "Not entirely, at least."

"All right. Turkey and cheese. And I want avocado on it too, with aioli, on the good bread."

"It's a deal."

Half an hour later, Lacy and Hannah had finished their sandwiches and were walking into the library. Evangeline Cooke, the head librarian, greeted them from behind the checkout counter.

"Hi, Hannah. How are you feeling, Lacy?"

"Big. I can't believe I still have three months to go," Lacy said. "But pretty good overall."

"Babies are such a blessing. I'm so happy for you guys."

"Thank you," Lacy said.

"Anything I can help you find?"

"We're looking for some old newspaper articles," Hannah said.

"You know how to find them?"

"I think so," Hannah said. She'd dug around in the digital archives a few times before. "I'll let you know if we have any trouble."

Evangeline waved, and Hannah led Lacy to the computer terminals. They settled in front of an open screen, and Hannah scooted her chair closer as Lacy opened the archive and typed in the search terms, *Witherspoon Museum theft.*

"Do we want to start by finding newspaper articles from the time?" Lacy asked.

"I think so," Hannah said, and Lacy limited the search parameters to the year 1990.

ART THEFT AT WITHERSPOON STUNS FRANKFORT, PRIORCELESS ART MISSING

Police were summoned to the Thomas G. Witherspoon Museum at 7:13 a.m. Thursday morning, responding to a call from museum guards who reported for their shift and found the night guard tied up. The night guard, Albert Johnston, told his coworkers that thieves had broken into the museum around 12:30 the previous night and tied him up at gunpoint. Upon examination, the guards discovered that the thieves had walked away with ten pieces of art by American masters, collectively worth hundreds of millions of dollars. Police are reviewing the security footage in the galleries.

The Witherspoon Museum is a private collection owned by Rockwell G. Witherspoon, and is open to the public six days per week. The collection was started by Rockwell's grandfather, Thomas, a great supporter of the arts, and subsequent generations of the family have added to the collection over the years. The museum was opened in 1977 to showcase the impressive collection and to make it available to the public for education and entertainment. "My family has always believed art is meant to be shared," Rockwell said. "This theft is a terrible violation of our trust, and we are shocked and horrified."

"These thieves have perpetrated a terrible crime," said Montgomery Carlyle, chair of the board of the Witherspoon Museum. "The stolen artworks are important pieces of the American canon and are extremely valuable. If anyone has any information about this theft, I beg you to report it to the police at once."

"There's not a lot of new information there," Lacy said.

Hannah studied the photo that accompanied the article. It showed a three-story brick building with large windows and a tiled roof. A caption underneath the photo identified it as the Witherspoon Museum. "It looks like a nice building, at least."

"This must be a follow-up," Lacy said, opening the next article on the screen. It had been published the next day.

Police Eye Security Guard, Mobsters, in Museum Theft

In the wake of the shocking theft at the Thomas G. Witherspoon Museum on Wednesday night, police are looking for suspects, and one name that keeps rising to the top is Albert Johnston, the night security guard who was working at the museum at the time of the theft.

Johnston is shown in security camera footage letting the two thieves in through the side entrance right before they tied him up. Museum protocol prohibited Johnston from letting anyone into the building during the overnight hours, but Johnston claims that the two men told him they were police officers and demanded entrance to the museum. Johnston insists he believed he was complying with the orders of Frankfort police when he opened the museum door and that he knew nothing about the thieves.

However, authorities have not ruled out the possibility that Johnston was working with the thieves, according to Sheriff Warren Fleming. When questioned about a possible connection at a press conference, Fleming says they are looking into Johnston's employment history and connections. "We are examining all possibilities," Fleming said. Johnston was hired two months before the theft.

Fleming also confirmed in the press conference that the police are exploring the possibility of organized crime. "It has come to our attention that there may be a reason to suspect a family known to the police," Fleming said. When pressed, he refused to elaborate further.

"We are examining all possibilities," Fleming repeated, just before shutting down the press conference.

"Oh my goodness." Lacy's hand flew to her mouth.

Hannah smiled, thinking she'd picked out the snippet that had elicited such a response from Lacy. She'd only learned about the mob in Kentucky a few months before while investigating another mystery. "Mobsters in Kentucky? Seems a bit hard to believe. Maybe if we were talking about Chicago or—"

"No, it's not that," Lacy said. "Look." She pointed at the photo that accompanied the article. It showed a man whom the caption identified as Albert Johnston, the security guard who was on duty at the time of the theft. "That's Uncle Al."

Hannah narrowed her eyes at the photo. "Who?"

"I thought it was a weird coincidence when you read his name from the first article," Lacy said. "But I didn't think it was him. I mean, Albert Johnston must be a pretty common name. But that picture is definitely him."

Hannah tried to catch up. "You know this guy?"

Lacy nodded. "We always called him Uncle Al, but he's really my dad's cousin. We didn't see him very often, because he lived in—well, he lived in Frankfort, actually. Which I guess makes sense now that I know he worked at the museum."

"You're sure that's your dad's cousin?" Hannah studied the photo. It was a grainy black-and-white picture, but it showed a man with curly hair, a mustache, round cheeks, a pointed chin, and dark eyes.

"Positive. I met him several times over the years. I can't believe I didn't know what had happened to him. Can you believe he was the guard who was tied up by the thieves?"

Hannah tried not to jump to conclusions, but something bothered her, something she wasn't sure she wanted to say out loud.

"No one ever said anything about this," Lacy said. "I mean, why would they, right? Would it really come up at a family gathering that your cousin was a suspect in a major art theft? But still. I can't believe I never knew."

"Is he still around?" Hannah asked.

"No, he passed away a decade or so ago. Dad went to his funeral, but I had finals. They were pretty close when they were young, I think."

Again, that thought at the back of her mind surfaced. She tried to push it away, but she couldn't quite get there.

"Lacy, do you think there's any chance…" Hannah tried to figure out how to ask tactfully. "That is, when we were talking to your mom earlier, she kind of acted like…I mean, do you think there's any chance she thought your dad might have known?"

"Known? About the paintings? No way." Lacy shook her head vehemently, and then slightly less vehemently, and then stopped altogether. "Wait."

Hannah bit her tongue, waiting for Lacy to catch up.

"She was a bit weird about that, wasn't she?" Lacy finally said. "Like really insistent that my dad couldn't have known the paintings were hidden in the cottage."

"Which, to be fair, he probably didn't."

"But he would have known that his cousin was a suspect," Lacy said. "He must have known that. It was all over the news."

"I'm sure he did know that," Hannah agreed. She had to let Lacy arrive at her own conclusions, just as Lacy would do for Hannah if the situation were reversed.

"And it does seem like a pretty amazing coincidence that the paintings turned up at the cottage my dad owned, when his cousin was the security guard at the museum who was suspected of involvement with the theft," Lacy said.

"Maybe your dad didn't know," Hannah said, feeling the need to reassure Lacy. "It's totally possible Albert hid the paintings at the cottage, but your dad never knew they were there, like your mom said."

"How would he have done that?" Lacy asked. "Torn down a wall in the kitchen, slipped the paintings inside, and sealed it back up, without Dad ever knowing? It doesn't seem very likely, does it?"

Hannah had to admit that it didn't. "Unless he was one of the people who stayed in the cottage for a short period of time. That's possible. After all, your mom said that they never went into the cottage when someone was staying there."

"But why would Mom be so cagey about it, if that were the case? She might not remember everyone who stayed in that cottage, but surely she would have remembered if one of the cops' primary suspects had been where the paintings were found. It doesn't seem like the kind of thing you'd forget to mention."

"Probably not," Hannah had to admit. She thought for a moment. "Maybe she wasn't sure if your dad knew about the paintings or not. She must have known Albert had been accused, but those paintings showing up at the cottage must have been a shock for her. Perhaps she was trying to make sure your dad wasn't considered a suspect."

"But she didn't mention the connection." Lacy shook her head. "That's what makes it feel weird, doesn't it? Why didn't she mention it, unless she was trying to hide something?"

"I don't know," Hannah said. "But it sounds like we have some more questions for your mom."

"I'm going to call her right now," Lacy said, and pushed herself up.

"Why don't we take a minute to think about it?" Hannah suggested. She wanted answers as much as Lacy did, but Lacy was upset, and now might not be the best time for her to talk to her mom.

"No. I'm calling her now," Lacy said, and Hannah saw that she'd already found her mom's contact. "We are getting to the bottom of this, no matter what."

Chapter Six

Hannah held her breath as they listened to the phone ring once, twice, three times.

"She's not picking up," Lacy said in frustration.

"I bet she's busy," Hannah said. "I'm sure she'll call you back."

"Or she's screening her calls," Lacy said. "She's avoiding me."

"I think that's a bit of a leap," Hannah said gently. "She's probably completely overwhelmed, given what she's just learned about what was hidden in a house on the family farm all this time."

"She should still pick up when her pregnant daughter calls," Lacy said petulantly.

"I'm sure she'll call you back as soon as she can." Hannah used her most soothing tone of voice. "In the meantime, let's see if there is any other information in the newspaper articles."

Lacy made a noise of frustration, but she returned to the computer and clicked on the next article in the list.

This one didn't have any new details, but it reiterated that the security guard on duty and organized crime were both possibilities that were being explored, and it also gave the full list of artists whose works had been stolen: Winslow Homer, Edward Hopper, Georgia O'Keefe, Andy Warhol, Mary Cassatt, Mark Rothko, Roy Lichtenstein, Thomas Cole, Edward Hicks, and John Singer Sargent. There were photographs of each of the paintings as well.

Hannah recognized the curved shapes and natural subject that indicated an O'Keefe, the pop-art style of the Lichtenstein, the solid blocks of color characteristic of a Rothko. The Cassatt was a sweet painting of a mother and child, and the Hopper showed a lonely night scene in some unnamed city. They were, according to a quote from the director of the museum, the ten most valuable and important works in the collection.

"That collection was no joke," Hannah said. "This Witherspoon guy managed to collect works from some of the most important American artists."

"And to think, thieves were able to just waltz in and steal paintings by the big names," Lacy said, shaking her head.

"I mean, that fact doesn't really help your cousin's case, if I'm honest," Hannah said. "That does make it seem like this could have been an inside job. That someone who was intimately familiar with the museum and its collection was involved in the theft."

"True," Lacy said. "Though if there was an inside person, it wasn't necessarily Albert. Anyone at the museum—the employees, the owners, even the people on the board—would have known which were the most important pieces."

"I imagine the police talked to all of them," Hannah said.

"I would hope so," Lacy said. "But maybe we can find out for sure."

Hannah leaned back in her chair. "On the other hand, the fact that it was such a professional job could also lend weight to the idea that it was, well, a professional job."

"You mean the mob?" Lacy smiled. "The infamous Kentucky mobsters, known for—what? Bluegrass and horses?"

"Yeah. It doesn't sound especially likely, does it?" Hannah said. She remembered her own incredulous reaction when her father had first told her the story during a previous investigation.

Before she could explain, Evangeline joined them. "Are you all finding everything you need?"

Lacy let out a long breath. "I don't know about that, honestly. Hannah was trying to convince me that there's a Kentucky Mafia that's responsible for an art heist."

"When was this crime?" Evangeline asked.

"In 1990," Lacy said.

Evangeline's expression grew pensive. "I know it sounds strange, but the Kentucky mob is no joke. Or it wasn't, anyway. Have you ever heard of Newport?"

"I know it's a city up north," Lacy said. "I've never been there, though."

"There's not a lot going on there these days," Evangeline said. "But decades ago, there was. Gambling was legal there, and all kinds of things happened in Newport. It was Las Vegas before Las Vegas. The name Sin City originally referred to Newport. And organized crime was certainly a part of it."

"Seriously?" Lacy asked. "Hannah, did you know about this?"

"Not as much as Evangeline, but yes, I'd heard something about it," Hannah said.

"I believe you, but I want to see for myself." Lacy switched over to a browser window and typed in *Newport, Kentucky*. The first thing that came up was an article from a magazine titled, "This Town Could Have Been Las Vegas."

"It's fascinating, really," Evangeline said. "You can read all about it, but the upshot is that mobsters from Cleveland came down and set up Newport to be a place where drinking and gambling were legal in the South. Organized crime thrived in Newport. The mob controlled the police, elections—all of it. It was just like the movies."

"What happens in Newport stays in Newport?" Lacy laughed at her own joke, and Hannah had to crack a smile. "So what happened?"

"They eventually went too far," Evangeline said. "A politician was framed for a crime because the mob wanted their own guy to win the election. The federal government got involved, and they shut it all down. They chased the mobsters and the illicit activities away. Realizing the game was over here, people headed west and settled in a little strip of desert called Las Vegas instead."

"When was this?"

"Early sixties, I think?" Evangeline said. "Somewhere around there. So most of the organized crime was gone by 1990, but I suspect it's the kind of thing that's hard to eradicate completely." She crossed her arms over her chest. "What exactly are you girls researching, anyway?"

"There was a theft at an art museum in Frankfort in 1990," Hannah explained. "Ten masterworks by American artists were taken, and most have never been recovered."

"I remember hearing about that. It was a big deal. They never did find out what happened, did they?"

"No," Lacy said. Hannah waited to see if she would mention that two of the paintings had recently turned up, or explain why they were interested in learning about this, but Lacy didn't, and Hannah decided to follow suit. After all, it was Lacy's story to tell, not hers.

"Some of the articles we've been reading indicate that the police suspected there might be a mob connection," Hannah said.

"I would say that if the police were looking at an organized crime connection, they probably had good reason to do so," Evangeline said. "I don't know how prevalent it was by that time, but I can say for certain that for a while, the mob was in Kentucky."

"So how would we find out more about that?" Hannah asked. She had a general idea about the situation, but more information never hurt.

"I don't know." Lacy sighed. "I don't know any mobsters, sadly."

"Are you sure you want to find out?" Evangeline said. "I mean, if there really is a connection to organized crime, that's probably not the kind of thing you'd want to get mixed up with."

"Fair enough," Hannah said, but she thought Evangeline was probably worrying too much. They weren't going to get mixed up with the mob, just try to figure out if they had a connection to the theft. "I don't really know how we'd find out more about that anyway."

"For now, maybe we'd better see what else we can turn up here," Lacy said.

"I'll leave you girls to it," Evangeline said. "But let me know if you need help. By the way, I heard the news. Congratulations on your engagement, Hannah."

"Thank you."

"Can I see the ring?"

"Of course. It belonged to Liam's grandmother." Hannah held her hand out and admired the way the diamond caught the light.

"Do you know when the wedding will be?"

"Not yet," Hannah said. She and Liam really needed to start planning.

"Fortunately, it's not as if you have a deadline for it," Evangeline said. "Let me know if you need help."

"We will," Hannah promised, and Evangeline bustled back toward the front desk.

"I guess we need to dig into this mob thing a little more," Lacy said.

Hannah agreed, but she also wanted to look into another name that had come up this morning. "What if you work on that while I try to find out more about Geraldine Steele and her family?"

"Oh, good call. Let me know what you find out."

Hannah scooted to the next terminal over and opened up a search window. Her fingers hovered over the keys as she tried to figure out what to search for. She wanted to look up Geraldine's family and any possible connection to the Witherspoon Museum. But she would need to know Geraldine's maiden name for that, and she didn't. She thought for a moment, and finally just typed in the name *Geraldine Steele.*

The first link that popped up was a website for a nonprofit called the Carlyle Foundation, and Geraldine was listed as the Executive Director. There was a headshot of her, her brown hair curling around her shoulders, and beneath that, there was a bio that said she was the daughter of Montgomery Carlyle, founder of the Carlyle Foundation, which directed its philanthropic efforts to support the arts and arts education. Christine had said Geraldine's family was into art. Was this what she had meant—that Geraldine supported arts organizations? Or was there more to it than that?

Hannah went back to the search results and started clicking links. There was a mention of Geraldine in an article in the *Blackberry Valley Chronicle* about last spring's Garden Tour, with a picture of her standing next to Colin when he had been sworn in as sheriff. That was from around five years ago, judging by the date on the page.

There was a social media profile, where Geraldine posted pictures of her garden, her adorable beagle puppy, her artwork, and vacations she and Colin had taken. An additional post included a nice shot of the couple in Venice, another of them in front of the Eiffel Tower, a third by the craziest-looking church Hannah had ever seen, with towers that appeared as though they were made of melted wax. The caption identified it as the Sagrada Familia in Barcelona. Maybe Hannah would make it to Spain someday. For now, she wasn't sure how she had never noticed that Colin and Geraldine seemed to have more money than a sheriff might usually make.

So Geraldine had money. That was great to know, but it didn't actually get Hannah anywhere closer to a connection with the paintings. Geraldine was probably ten years older than Hannah, which meant that she would only have been a child in 1990 when the museum was broken into. She definitely couldn't have been involved in the heist. But Christine had said something about her family collecting art. So maybe Hannah needed to go back a bit further.

Hannah decided to research Geraldine's father. A search for the name *Montgomery Carlyle* returned an obituary. Montgomery had passed six years ago and was dearly missed by his family and friends. The article mentioned the Carlyle Foundation and…

Well, that's interesting.

Montgomery Carlyle had been on the board of the Witherspoon Museum. Actually, he'd been mentioned in one of the articles they'd just read, hadn't he? She clicked back to the article published the day after the theft and saw that he had indeed been quoted. He was the chair of the board, in fact. She just hadn't realized he was Geraldine's father when she'd first read it.

It could be a total coincidence that Geraldine's father had been the board chair of the museum the paintings were stolen from, and that two of the paintings had turned up in the house where Geraldine and Colin lived for a time.

Still, if there was any truth to the rumors that the theft had been an inside job, Montgomery was not a bad place to look.

Hannah was about to open her mouth to say as much to Lacy, but just then Lacy gasped. "Hannah, you'll never believe this."

Chapter Seven

I figured out why the police think the mob had something to do with the theft," Lacy said.

"Why?" Hannah asked.

"Well, apparently this guy Vinnie Amelio was known to be a big deal in the organized crime world in Newport—"

"Even though organized crime was supposedly shut down there in the sixties?"

"The gambling halls were shut down," Lacy clarified. "Apparently, it wasn't so easy to get rid of *all* the organized crime. This guy seems to have been known to the police, because right after the theft, they interviewed Amelio and tried to pin it on him, but he always denied any knowledge of the museum or the art heist."

The article on Lacy's screen showed a mug shot of a man with dark hair and eyes and a cocky grin.

"Does it say why they thought he was involved?"

"No. It looks like maybe law enforcement didn't want that information public or something. Or maybe there wasn't a clear reason, but he was somehow involved in everything bad that went down back then. This doesn't say. But he was definitely on their radar, and he's suspected of all kinds of terrible crimes. They were finally able to arrest him on charges of embezzling, around a year after the museum theft. When they searched his home, they found a list—in

Amelio's handwriting—of all the stolen paintings, as well as their value."

"Whoa. That doesn't look good."

"He again denied any wrongdoing, saying he'd heard of the theft and followed the news story, and was just curious as to the value of the paintings. Naturally, the police didn't believe him, but they couldn't prove anything."

"Were they ever able to prove a connection?"

"Nope," Lacy said. "He's been in prison for the last thirty-odd years."

"For embezzling?"

"That's what they started with, but it seems they've been able to verify several other crimes since then that have extended his sentence. Anyway, he's locked up, and they never got anything out of him regarding the paintings. But there does appear to be good reason to think organized crime might have been involved."

"I still think it's crazy that such things happen in Kentucky."

"Me too." Lacy sat forward. "Anyway, I also got distracted by the idea that another one of the paintings had been recovered, so I looked into that."

"What did you find?"

Lacy switched to a different tab and an article titled STOLEN ROTHKO RECOVERED appeared on the screen. The article was accompanied by a photograph of a painting made up of colored blocks. "It turns out this piece wasn't found hidden in a wall somewhere random."

"Which is obviously the most logical place to store art," Hannah quipped.

"Right." Lacy smiled. "But get this—the stolen Rothko was hanging on some guy's wall in New York City. He hosted a party and showed it off."

"What?" Hannah said. "He drew attention to his stolen artwork?"

"Apparently. That's what's so crazy. According to this article, most of the time when art gets stolen, it's never recovered."

"Yikes."

"I know. It ends up in 'private collections' and never sees the light of day again. But not this one. According to this article, ten years ago, a bigwig at some tech company threw a party for his executive team and their families in his Manhattan penthouse. A woman who worked at a gallery in Chelsea attended the party with her husband and saw the painting. She asked about it, and the host said it was a real Rothko and he'd had to pay a fortune for it, but it was worth it because he loved it so much. But the woman recognized the piece, and knew it had been stolen from a museum. She reported it to the police. The painting was recovered and returned to the Witherspoon Museum."

"Wow. I bet that employee was not very popular at work on Monday, after his wife called the cops on his boss. Did they ever figure out how it got from the gallery to that guy's wall?"

"This article doesn't say that they did, but I don't know. It's also not clear whether he knew the painting was stolen, which definitely impacts how I feel about him. Did he know he was buying a stolen painting and just not care? Or did he think he was spending millions on a legitimate painting only to be out all that money?"

Hannah couldn't imagine having enough money to buy a Rothko, legitimately or not. "At least one of the paintings did surface eventually," Hannah said. "But that was the only one, right?"

"Before today, yes."

"Wow. So now three of the ten have been recovered. But how did one go from the museum walls to a Manhattan penthouse, and two to a cottage in rural Kentucky?"

"I still have no clue," Lacy said with a sigh.

"I don't either." Hannah checked the time. She would have to leave soon. But first, she pulled a notepad and pen from her bag to make notes. "Okay. So what do we know?"

"We know that the security guard who let the thieves in was my dad's cousin, which makes it extra suspicious that two of the paintings ended up at our cottage."

"And I've learned that Geraldine Steele's family had a connection to the museum, and that she and the sheriff lived in the cottage for a while," Hannah said.

"What?" Lacy gaped at her.

Hannah filled her in on what she'd read.

"That's suspicious," Lacy said.

"Colin and Geraldine lived in the cottage fifteen years after the theft, so if they are behind it, we need to figure out where the paintings were in the meantime," Hannah added. "They must have been stashed somewhere else for all those years."

"That's true of anyone except whoever lived there at exactly the time of the theft," Lacy said. "So that's the second thing we know. And we know that the police believed there may have been a mob connection, which I can't get over."

"So where does that leave us?" Hannah asked. It seemed they weren't any closer to finding out what had happened than they had been before arriving at the library.

"Confused," Lacy said. "There's one other thing we know, though."

"What's that?"

"That you need to get going if you're going to make yourself look presentable before you meet your fiancé's parents for the first time."

Hannah laughed. "I guess that means we call it a day."

"For now. Don't worry, though. I'll keep digging. We'll figure this thing out."

When Hannah got home, her mind swirled with questions about what she and Lacy had discovered earlier and how the paintings had ended up in the cottage. She tried to turn them off while she did a little work in the restaurant office, then got ready to meet Liam and his parents. She had met Liam's grandfather, Patrick, many times. But his parents had moved to Florida, and while Liam had gone to see them, they hadn't been back to visit since she'd started dating him. She was excited to meet them now.

Excited, and more than a little nervous.

She played worship music as she painted her toenails and touched up her hair, and then as she ironed the light cotton dress she had picked out.

The Bertholds had to be nice people, Hannah told herself as she refreshed her makeup. They had raised Liam, who was the best person she knew. If they raised a son like him, they had to be all right. Plus, Liam's dad had been the fire chief before Liam. They had so much to talk about.

Still, Hannah said a prayer as she checked the mirror one last time and headed down the stairs. Hannah spent a big chunk of her time at the Hot Spot, the restaurant she'd opened when she moved home to Blackberry Valley, but she didn't often get to eat there as a guest. It felt unnatural to show up and sit in the dining room. But Liam had wanted to take his parents there to show off what he called "the best food in town."

She found Liam standing outside the restaurant, accompanied by two people with dark hair threaded with gray who had to be his parents.

"There she is," Liam said, and his parents turned toward her. They both smiled as they saw her, and Hannah felt something inside her relax. "You look beautiful," he said, leaning in to kiss her cheek as she got close. "Mom and Dad, this is Hannah Prentiss, the most amazing woman in the world. Hannah, meet my mom and my dad."

"I'm Daniel," his dad said, holding out his hand. He had the same brown eyes and strong jawline as his son, but wore glasses and was a few inches shorter.

"And I'm Lori," his mother said, pulling Hannah in for a hug. "It's wonderful to finally meet you. Liam has told us so much about you."

"It's great to meet you both," Hannah said. Lacy had been right. There was no reason to worry. "I'm so glad you came to visit."

"I've heard so much about your restaurant as well," Lori said. "I'm excited to finally get to eat here."

"The food is excellent," Liam said. "You'll love it."

"It's amazing that this is the old firehouse," Daniel said, gazing up at the brick building. "It looks totally different inside, but the outside has barely changed." Hannah had bought the firehouse after the new one was constructed, and turned the building into the Hot Spot.

"I tried to retain as much of the character of the old firehouse as I could," Hannah said. "It was important to me to honor the building for what it used to be."

Daniel laughed. "It used to be a place where a bunch of sweaty men spent too much time watching sports."

Liam grinned. "Well, the new firehouse is where a bunch of sweaty men spend too much time watching sports now. And this is the best restaurant in town. Shall we go inside?"

"I can't wait," Lori said, smiling brightly.

Liam rested his hand on Hannah's back as they started for the door. Daniel held the door open, and they walked inside.

"Wow," she heard Daniel say under his breath. "This is different."

"Hello," Elaine Wilby greeted them from the hostess stand. "Welcome to the Hot Spot."

"Hi, Elaine," Hannah said. "Can we have a table for four, please?"

"Of course. Right this way." Elaine took four menus from the bin and indicated that they should follow her. Hannah had warned the staff that she would be bringing Liam's parents in tonight, of course, and it looked like Elaine had reserved the best table in the house by the front window. When they were all seated, she handed out the menus, then winked at Hannah before returning to the hostess stand.

"Hannah, this is beautiful," Lori said. "I love how you kept some of the old memorabilia from the fire department as decorations."

She indicated the black-and-white photographs of firefighters from over the years, and an old fire hat.

"Thank you. Liam helped me with the decorations, actually."

"Gramps kept a lot of this old stuff," Liam said. "And he was happy to see it put on display."

"You've also made the place so warm and inviting. It certainly wasn't that way before," Lori said. "It's wonderful." She pulled reading glasses out of her purse and looked at her menu.

"You did all this by yourself?" Daniel asked.

"I had plenty of help. My dad is a retired electrician, and my uncle is a retired plumber, and they contributed a lot," Hannah said.

"Hannah worked in some high-end restaurants in Los Angeles, so she knows what she's doing when it comes to restaurants," Liam added with pride. "Just wait until you try the food."

"Technically the chef, Jacob Forrest, does most of the cooking," Hannah said. "He does a phenomenal job."

"But Hannah creates the menu and keeps it updated based on what's in season, though some things stay on the menu year-round. It's a farm-to-table restaurant, so she sources a lot of ingredients locally," Liam said. "And trust me—it's always delicious."

"What do you recommend?" Lori asked. "It all looks so good."

"The Five-Alarm Burger is probably our best-selling hamburger," Hannah said. "It has cream cheese, fried jalapeños, and raspberry-pepper jelly."

"It's amazing," Liam said.

"I can't do spicy," Daniel said. "How hot are the jalapeños?"

"Well, let's just say we don't call it Five-Alarm Burger for nothing," Hannah said, smiling. "In that case, you should probably try something else. The Rookie Meltdown just has pepperjack cheese. It's got a little kick to it, but not too much."

"He wants his food as mild as it comes," Liam said with a grin. "Dad, I think you'd like the Brushfire Steak. Jacob makes a mean steak, and the sauce it comes with is incredible."

"I've never turned down a good steak," Daniel said. "I'll have that."

"And maybe an order of wings to start," Lori said. "The least-spicy version."

"That would be the Glowing Embers," Hannah said.

"You really leaned into the fire theme," Lori said. "I guess that's why you had to marry a firefighter, huh?"

"Totally," Hannah said, laughing. "It didn't matter which one. I just needed a fireman to complete the theme. Good thing I got a good one."

Lori laughed, but Daniel wore a slight frown.

"I'm kidding," Hannah added quickly. "That's not why I'm marrying Liam."

Liam took her hand and smiled at her.

"What actually happened is that I was going broke eating here all the time," Liam said. "I came for the food, originally, but then I fell under the spell of the pretty owner, and soon I was spending all my time and money here. I figured I had to marry her to save money."

Daniel laughed at that. He could obviously tell Liam was joking. He'd known she was joking too, right? She glanced at Liam, who squeezed her hand.

She was grateful when server Raquel Holden walked up carrying a sizzling plate. "Good evening, and welcome to the Hot Spot.

We're so glad you're here tonight. The chef sent along this dish as a special treat as you get settled in." Raquel winked at Hannah as she slid a plate of Kentucky Hot Browns onto the table.

"Oh my goodness, I love these," Lori said.

"Please send our thanks to the chef," Hannah said. It was actually kind of nice to be here as a guest, she realized. They were pulling out all the stops to help her impress her future in-laws.

Raquel took everyone's drink order and walked away. Lori smiled and said, "Is that Melissa Holden's daughter? I haven't seen her in years. She's grown up so much."

"That's right," Hannah confirmed.

"Is she still dating that Coleman boy?" Lori asked. "I remember her mother did not like him."

"No, Raquel is dating Marshall Fredericks now," Liam said. "He used to work for *Blackberry Valley Chronicle*, but he recently moved to Chicago for a job. They're making it work long-distance."

"She's a wonderful person," Hannah added. "I'm lucky to have her."

Soon Raquel came with glasses of ice water for all of them and took their orders. Then they dug into the Hot Browns, which were essentially turkey breast on toast, topped with bacon and a Mornay sauce.

"Oh wow," Lori said, taking a bite. "That's really good. It might be the best of its kind I've ever had."

Hannah watched Daniel, hoping he liked the dish as well, but his face didn't reveal anything. Did he like it? Did he like her? He was so quiet that it was hard to tell what he was thinking.

"So, Hannah, tell us, what made you move back to Blackberry Valley?" Lori asked.

Hannah told them how she'd moved to Los Angeles for college and worked at restaurants out there, but after her mom passed away, she'd worried about her dad more and more. She'd also gotten tired of spending so much time commuting in her car in Los Angeles, and she'd always wanted to open her own restaurant. Moving home seemed like the best way to address all of those things.

"Blackberry Valley really is the best place to live, isn't it?" Lori said. "We miss it here, much as we love our life in Florida." She nudged Liam. "Your dad has taken up pickleball. Can you believe it?"

"I would love to see that," Liam said, eyes twinkling. "You chasing that little ball all over the court."

"It's good exercise," Daniel said. "And we have a group that always goes out for a meal afterward."

"They immediately replace all the calories they just burned," Lori joked.

Daniel turned to Hannah. "Do you play any sports?"

"Me? Oh, no. I've never been coordinated enough, sadly." She could sense that the answer wasn't what Daniel wanted to hear, so she quickly added, "But I like watching sports."

"What sports do you follow?"

She realized in that moment that she'd made a mistake.

"I mean, I don't really *follow* any," she said. "Not exactly." What was she supposed to say? Some people around here rooted for the St. Louis Rams or the Nashville Predators. What team did Liam root for? She was pretty sure he was a Pittsburgh Steelers fan, for some reason she'd never understood.

Daniel watched her in silence, as if waiting for her to explain.

Hannah decided to come clean. "I really like watching ice-skating and gymnastics during the Olympics," she said. "And I've gone to a few baseball games. Baseball doesn't move so fast, so you can chat with your friends during the game without missing anything."

The way Liam's father looked at her—like she was speaking a foreign language or was totally nuts—made her realize she'd once again said the wrong thing.

"I don't really watch much ice-skating," he said slowly. "Do you ever watch football?"

She took a breath and let it out slowly. She was beginning to feel like she couldn't get it right, no matter what she said. "Not a lot, but my dad and my uncle often have a game on, so I sometimes watch when I'm at their place."

By that, she meant she would sometimes catch a glimpse of the screen when she went in to tell them dinner was ready, but she didn't need to admit that here.

Liam squeezed her hand under the table, and she appreciated it, but it didn't change the fact that she was messing up this whole thing, just as she'd feared. She'd wanted so badly to impress his parents and to get to know them, and suddenly it felt like nothing she did was right.

This was not going at all the way she'd hoped.

Chapter Eight

After dinner, Hannah went upstairs and took a long, hot shower. Lori was sweet, but no matter how hard she'd tried, she seemed unable to connect with Daniel. Still, they'd hugged her and said they were excited to see her again soon. Liam had kissed her and murmured that she'd done well, but he was probably just trying to make her feel better.

She tossed and turned that night, reliving what felt like some major missteps in the conversation interspersed with questions about the paintings in the cottage. Though she finally drifted off, her sleep was restless.

The next morning, Hannah made coffee and got ready for church, and the bright sunshine of a beautiful May morning lifted her spirits. The rich smell of the coffee filling the apartment also helped. She made herself eggs and toast for breakfast, then spent some time reading her Bible. She flipped to Isaiah, looking for the passage that had inspired the Edward Hicks painting. She found it in chapter 11.

> *The wolf will live with the lamb,*
> *the leopard shall lie down with the goat,*
> *the calf and the lion and the yearling together;*
> *and a little child shall lead them.*
> *The cow will feed with the bear,*
> *their young will lie down together,*

and the lion will eat straw like the ox.
The infant will play near the cobra's den,
and the young child will put its hand into the viper's nest.
They will neither harm nor destroy
on all my holy mountain,
for the earth will be filled with the knowledge of the LORD
as the waters cover the sea.

It was a beautiful image, one of peace, where even natural enemies gave up fighting and rested together in harmony.

After she'd read the passage through a couple times, she reviewed the notes in her Bible about the book of Isaiah itself. Isaiah was one of the most important prophetic books in the Bible, written while the remnant of Israel was in exile under Assyrian rule. Isaiah had spent the chapters leading up to this passage calling down condemnation on the powerful armies that ruled the land and kept God's people in captivity, but in this chapter, the text turned to looking toward the Savior the Lord had promised His people. Toward the shoot from the stump of Jesse, who would be filled with wisdom and understanding, and bring such an extraordinary peace that all creatures—and all nations—would live in serenity together.

That shoot from the stump of Jesse was, of course, Jesus, prophesied all those years ago. He had come to redeem His people. So why didn't it feel like the world was at peace? Why was it so hard to understand even the people sitting across from her sometimes?

Last night's dinner being Exhibit A.

Lord, help me to bring peace and understanding today, she prayed. Then she got up and left for church.

The sun shone on fresh green leaves, making the world feel lush and beautiful. Hannah thanked the Lord for spring sunshine as she parked in the lot behind Grace Community Church. She saw Liam's car, Dad's, and many others she recognized. No matter what else was happening, she was glad she could spend the morning worshipping the Lord with her church family.

She found Liam in a pew near the front, and she slid in next to him.

"Where are your parents?" she asked, looking over at him. He really was very handsome. Sometimes she still couldn't believe she got to be with this man, and that he had chosen her.

Liam took her hand and squeezed it. "Catching up," he said. He gestured toward the back of the church. She turned and saw that they were indeed talking animatedly with Joe Wilson, the owner of Blackberry Market.

"I bet they're excited to see so many old friends," Hannah said.

"Definitely. They spent so much time in this church," Liam said. "When I was a kid, I thought it was far too much time, honestly, but I appreciate it now."

Feeling the warmth of his arm against hers, she appreciated it too. Lori and Daniel—and all they had done to raise their son in faith—were a big part of the reason he had become the man he was today. She was and would always be grateful to them for that.

"What are you smiling about?" Liam asked.

"Just thinking how blessed I am," Hannah said.

Uncle Gordon stepped into the empty row in front of them and turned to Hannah. "I heard a rumor about the old cottage on Bluegrass Hollow Farm. Did you really find old paintings in the wall?"

"We really did," Hannah said. "Well, Liam did."

"I almost smashed them with my sledgehammer, truth be told," Liam said. "Luckily we spotted them before any damage was done."

"I have so many questions," Uncle Gordon said as the opening notes of the first hymn played.

"You and me both. I want to ask you about a few things as well," Hannah said.

"It sounds like we don't have time to talk right now," Uncle Gordon said. "Your dad and I are headed over to Maeve's for lunch after church. Why don't you come along too?"

"Do you think that would be okay with her?" Maeve was Uncle Gordon's daughter and Hannah's cousin, but Hannah didn't want to just show up uninvited.

"Of course it's okay. Maeve won't mind. She always cooks for an army anyway."

Liam and his parents were going to visit Daniel's father, Patrick, after church, and tonight his parents were having dinner with the Dawsons while Liam worked. Tomorrow they were all going on a hike. But for today, she didn't have any real plans except digging into this mystery.

Still. "Maybe I should talk to her after church."

"I'll let her know you're coming. Can you come too, Liam?" Uncle Gordon asked. "Bring your parents. I'd love to catch up with them."

"Unfortunately, we can't today," Liam said. "Though I know they'd love to meet up with you while they're in town."

"We'll have to make that happen." Uncle Gordon started to walk toward his seat, and Liam's parents came and slid into the pew next to their son.

Soon the congregation was singing "Great Is Thy Faithfulness," and Hannah lost herself in the words and the reminder that God was in control, no matter what.

Hannah stopped by Sweet Caroline's Bakery and picked up a loaf of crusty French bread on the way to Maeve's house after church. Hannah had talked to her cousin after the service, and Maeve let her know she was more than welcome. "I've got questions about that cottage too," Maeve had said, before turning to wrangle seven-year-old Paxton off the back of the pew. "See you soon!"

When Hannah stepped into Maeve's house, she found Dad and Uncle Gordon watching a baseball game on TV and her cousin Ryder hunched over a game of Monopoly with Rory and Sutton, Maeve's girls. Maeve's husband, Hunter, was out in the yard playing basketball with Paxton.

"Monopoly? You're a brave man," Hannah said to Ryder. "You might be here all week."

"We started this game last time I was here," Ryder said. "And it's still going. But I've built hotels on the yellows, so I have a feeling it will be over soon enough."

"That's what he thinks," thirteen-year-old Sutton quipped, holding up the deed to Boardwalk.

"Good luck with that," Hannah said, and walked on through to the kitchen, where she found Maeve holding a steaming colander of pasta over the sink. Hannah spotted a pan with tomato sauce and sautéed eggplant on the stove, and grated ricotta salata on the counter.

"Pasta alla Norma?" Hannah asked.

"That's it. If I bathe the eggplant in enough olive oil, the kids don't realize they're eating vegetables," Maeve said. "Thanks for bringing bread. We're about ready to eat."

It took a few minutes to gather everyone and get them settled around the table.

After Hunter said a prayer and everyone had been served, Uncle Gordon turned to Hannah. "So what's the story with the cottage? I've heard all kinds of rumors about what you found there, but I want to know what's real."

"What have you heard?" Hannah asked, spearing a bite of eggplant and penne. "And where did you hear it?"

"Wyatt Granger told me that there was a painting by Picasso found behind the shower in the cottage on the Johnston property," Uncle Gordon said. Wyatt was a town councilman and served as the head of the local business association.

"I heard that it was two paintings, and they were stolen from the Louvre Museum in Paris," Maeve added. "Which seemed a bit far-fetched to me."

"Colt Walker said tools were stolen from the cottage but didn't say anything about paintings being found," Ryder added.

"Wow." Hannah held up her hands. "Okay. There's some misinformation there. First of all, Colt is right. Tools were stolen from the cottage. However, the paintings were found inside a wall in the kitchen. They were paintings by two important American artists, though I hadn't previously heard of either one of them." She pulled up pictures of the two paintings on her phone and passed it around the table so they could all look. "Edward Hicks and Thomas Cole.

But both paintings were stolen from an art museum in Frankfort in 1990."

"Wait. You mean *that* big break-in?" Dad asked. "The guys who tied up the security guard?"

"That's the one," Hannah said.

"It was all over the news," Uncle Gordon said. "They thought the mob was involved, didn't they?"

"That is one theory," Hannah said.

"How in the world did paintings that were stolen from a museum get into the Johnstons' cottage?" Uncle Gordon asked.

"Were the paintings hidden inside when we lived there?" Maeve asked.

"We don't know any of that," Hannah said. "That's kind of what I wanted to ask you about. I want to talk to people who lived in the cottage over the years to see what they remember."

"I remember that place was creepy," Maeve said. She looked at the pictures, swiping the screen to see both paintings, then handed the phone to Hunter. "I didn't like it."

"It wasn't creepy. It was just small," Ryder said.

"It was creepy, set out there in the woods with no one around. Anyone could have come around and gotten in, and there was no one to hear you scream." Maeve shuddered. "Plus the water heater barely worked, and the roof leaked. I know you liked it because you could wander around in the woods all day long, and you loved that. But not all of us were happy there."

"Wandering around in the woods is one of my favorite things," Ryder said. "But I can see why you didn't like it there. The cottage was small, and it was a long drive to see your friends."

"It wasn't our home," Maeve insisted. "And it was a long drive to everything. Work, school, friends—all of it. But mostly, it just wasn't home."

"I'm sorry, once again, for accidentally setting the fire," Ryder said, in a tone that conveyed that this wasn't the first time he'd apologized for the same thing. "I didn't do it on purpose."

"We know that," Uncle Gordon cut in. "And this conversation isn't about that. What Hannah wants to know is whether any of us remembers anything that might help discover who left the paintings there. And the answer is no. If they were hidden in the cottage during the time we lived there, none of us were aware." He took the phone from Hunter and studied the photos before passing the device to Hannah's dad.

"When did you live there?" Hannah asked.

"2008," Maeve said. "I remember because I was going to community college and working at the daycare, and I thought about getting a place of my own instead of staying in that cottage, but I was trying to save up to transfer, so it didn't really make sense."

"It was my senior year of high school," Ryder said. "It wasn't exactly how I intended to spend it either."

"Maybe you should have thought of that before you tried to deep-fry a candy bar," Maeve teased.

"I was hungry. And it would have been awesome if it had all gone according to plan."

"That does sound good," Sutton said. "Can I try that sometime?"

"No," both of her parents said in unison.

"Did you miss the part where your uncle burned the house down trying it?" Maeve asked.

"All right," Uncle Gordon said. "That's enough. It was an accident, one your brother has apologized for many times. If you've never made a mistake, feel free to keep nagging your brother."

Maeve looked at her pasta, chastened. "Sorry, Ryder."

"It's okay."

"*Luckily*, no one was hurt," Uncle Gordon said, with a tone of finality in his voice. "Daniel Berthold got his men there in minutes, and they contained the fire to the kitchen. The rest of the house just had smoke damage. I'll never stop being grateful to them for what they did to save the day. I told him so again when I saw him this morning, in fact."

"Hey, Hannah, how'd it go meeting the parents?" Maeve asked, smiling again.

Hannah didn't really want to get into that right now. "Fine, I guess. But can we go back to the cottage? So, none of you knew the paintings were in the walls while you lived there?"

"Fine, as long as we get back to that at some point." Maeve winked at her.

"That's right," Uncle Gordon said. "If they were there in 2008, none of us knew it. But if they were found behind a wall, they could have been there for who knows how long."

"Christine Johnston told me that while you lived there you did some repair work in the kitchen," Hannah said. "And you had to open up a wall."

"That's true," Uncle Gordon said. "During an especially cold spell, one of the pipes that went to the sink burst while we were all out one day. It hadn't been installed correctly and was too close to the exterior wall. We came home and found water on the floor."

"A fire and a flood, all in the space of a few months," Maeve said.

"There is no way this one was my fault," Ryder added.

"Frank came over and helped us clean it all up, and he understood that it wasn't anything we'd done wrong. I told him that to bring the plumbing up to code, we'd need to tear out all the pipes along that wall and reinstall them. He gave us a deal on the rent because I handled that for him."

"Which wall was this?" Hannah asked, trying to picture the little kitchen in the cottage. "The one that faces the yard, right?" That was where the sink was. The exterior wall where they'd found the paintings faced the woods and the hills.

"Exactly." Uncle Gordon took a bite of bread. "I wish I had known the paintings were there, to be honest. I've never heard of those two artists you mentioned, but the pictures are pretty. Elyse would have liked them." Elyse was his late wife.

"So how *did* the paintings get there?" Dad asked, cocking his head. "And when?"

"I don't know," Hannah said. "Hopefully we can find out."

"But here's what I don't get," Hunter said. "Why were the pictures there at all? If someone knew they were there and they're as valuable as you say, why wouldn't someone have sold them rather than hide them away all this time?"

"Where does one sell stolen paintings? Especially ones that have been all over the news?" Dad asked.

"I don't know," Hunter said. "But presumably whoever broke into the museum and took them would."

"Someone did," Hannah confirmed. "We know because one of the stolen paintings was recovered many years later, and someone had paid a lot of money for it. So there is certainly a lucrative black market for stolen art."

"Well, I don't have any clue how to access that black market," Uncle Gordon said. "But Hunter's point stands. Why were these paintings hidden where, presumably, they would never be found, instead of sold?"

"That's another question I'm hoping to answer," Hannah said.

"Can we talk about how those paintings aren't the only thing strange going down at that cottage these days?" Ryder said. "Let's not forget that Gus Brody's tools were stolen. They were brought over the night before demo started, and someone broke in and took them."

"That's right," Hannah said. In the wake of the discovery of the paintings, she kept forgetting about the tools.

"What kind of tools were they?" Uncle Gordon asked.

"A power saw, I think," Hannah said. "And a toolbox. I assume there were tools in there, but I don't know what. A sledgehammer."

"Colt said there was stuff there that wasn't taken too, like a cannister vacuum and some copper wire," Ryder said.

"Thefts like this are more common these days, now that anyone can sell anything anonymously online," Uncle Gordon said, shaking his head.

"How does Colt know all this?" Hannah asked.

"Gus Brody is his uncle," Ryder said. "But listen. Don't you think it's odd that the thief left the vacuum and the wire behind? And only took the tools?"

Hannah shrugged. "Why does anyone steal anything? Maybe they just needed some tools."

"The tools are valuable," Dad said. "But the copper wire is more valuable. Copper is in high demand, and you can get real money for it. Much more so than a used table saw."

"Even if the thief didn't need copper, most people would have taken it to sell," Hunter said. "If money was a motive, anyway."

"Okay." Hannah tried to wrap her mind around this. It seemed like all the men in her family saw something that she didn't. "So what do you think is going on?"

"There's a chance the thief simply didn't know how valuable copper wire is," Uncle Gordon started, but the way he said it, it was clear he didn't believe his own words.

"But if they only ended up taking the tools and left behind the most valuable stuff, you start to wonder if it was really about money," Dad said.

"As in, the things that were taken were the tools needed to open the wall," Hunter said. "Like maybe someone knew what was there, and knew you would find it, and wanted to try to stop that from happening."

"Oh." Hannah now saw what they were getting at.

"No one motivated by cash would take a sledgehammer and leave a roll of copper wire," Dad said.

Hannah saw his point. "Do you really think it's possible?" If the break-in had been instigated as a way to try to stop them from starting renovations and finding the paintings—that meant someone out there knew the pieces were still hidden inside the walls.

Someone knew they were still there and had wanted to make sure they weren't found.

Chapter Nine

After Hannah helped Maeve clean up lunch, she headed home, an idea forming in her mind. Uncle Gordon mentioned that thefts had become more common because so many things could be sold anonymously online these days. Was there any chance…?

But the moment she walked in the door, her phone rang. She pulled it out and answered when she read the name on the screen. "Hey, Lacy," she said, setting her bag on the table by the door.

"Hi. You ran out so quickly after the service that I didn't have time to find out how last night went."

"It was fine."

"Fine? What does that mean?"

Hannah kicked off her shoes and walked over to the couch, flopping down on the cushions. "I don't know. Liam's mom is so nice. She's really lovely, and I like her a lot."

"And his dad?"

"He was nice too. But he was kind of hard to read. He didn't say a lot. And when he did, it felt like every answer I gave was the wrong one."

"Example?"

"Like, I made a joke about how I had to marry a firefighter because of the theme of my restaurant, but I'm not sure he knew I was kidding. And he asked whether I liked sports, and seemed really disappointed when I said no. Well, actually, I said yes, and then had to backtrack and say I meant ice-skating, not football, and then it was really awkward."

"I bet he was as nervous as you were."

"What does he have to be nervous about? I'm not intimidating in the least."

"You're marrying their son. He is important to them, so they want you to like them."

"*I* want *them* to like *me*."

"And you're just getting to know each other. Give it time. You'll learn how to interact with him."

"I don't know."

"Trust me on this one. When I first met Neil's parents, they thought I was this silly farm girl, and they didn't see why their serious son was interested in me. But as we got to know each other, we found things we have in common, and we built a relationship. And it will get better for you, I promise."

"I hope you're right."

"I'm always right."

Hannah laughed and put her feet up on her coffee table.

"Anyway, here's some different parent drama. Did you notice my mom wasn't in church today?" Lacy said.

"No," Hannah admitted. She'd been too wrapped up in the paintings and Liam's parents. "Why did she miss it?"

"I didn't know, so I called her to make sure everything was okay. But she didn't pick up her phone."

"Is she okay?" A weird strain of the flu had been going around town recently.

"She finally called me back after I'd called her twice. She said she's fine, just wanted to sleep in this morning. That's not like her at all, so I knew something was up."

"Did you find out what?"

"She didn't say, but when I asked her why she hadn't mentioned that Dad's cousin was the security guard on duty at the museum the night of the theft, she got really quiet. I pushed her, and she asked if we could talk in person. So she's coming over for dinner tonight. You should come too, if you don't have plans."

"Would I be intruding? This sounds like a family thing."

"You're basically family. Besides, if she knows something about the theft or the paintings, you need to be there to hear it too. We're investigating this together."

She did want to hear what Christine had to say and find out why she hadn't said it before. "Liam has to work, and his parents are having dinner with the Dawsons. I was going to catch up on some shows."

"Perfect. See you at six?"

"Can I bring a key lime pie?"

"You know me so well."

"See you later."

Hannah went to the kitchen to get started on the pie. As she gathered the ingredients, she decided to find the podcast Margot had mentioned, the one that talked about the Witherspoon robbery. It was called *A Brush with Danger*, and it started with the host, Sarah Smalley, announcing her intention to find out what had really happened the night of the museum theft.

Having listened to true crime podcasts before, Hannah recognized the format—the host gave an intriguing summary of what had taken place, then promised to explore all the nuances and tell the inside story that had never been told. Sarah Smalley had hosted similar podcasts in the past, and her work was well-edited, well-written, and utterly fascinating. Hannah listened to the first episode as she squeezed the limes and made the custard.

Sarah set the scene at the museum and explained what had happened. She interviewed one of the police officers who had been called to the scene as well as one of the guards who had found security guard Albert Johnston tied up the next morning. By the end of the first episode, Hannah hadn't learned anything she didn't already know, but she was riveted and couldn't wait to hear more.

Once the pie was chilling in the fridge, she decided to look into something Uncle Gordon said that had been nagging at her. She sat down in front of her computer and opened a web browser, then she typed in the name of an online auction company. She searched for *table saw* and limited her search parameters to within twenty-five miles of her location. Two results turned up. What kind of table saw was she looking for? She had no idea. Wait, one of these said it was *new in box*. That probably wasn't it, but could the other one be Gus's table saw that someone was trying to sell? Hannah had no way to tell.

Okay, maybe this wouldn't go anywhere. She typed in *toolbox* with the same parameters, just to see, but that didn't turn up anything more useful. There were three toolboxes that popped up, but none were from the same seller as either table saw. Since she didn't know exactly what she was looking for, she didn't know what to make of any of it. She tried the same searches again on the Buy and Sell page of a social media site, but didn't come up with anything.

Closing that window, Hannah returned to the main search page, but she didn't even know what to look for. Her fingers hovered over the keys. The police had investigated the possibility of organized crime, but she didn't know how she would find out more about that. Still, the security guard was one possible link between the thefts and the cottage. She would ask Christine about that tonight.

Another possible connection between the cottage and the museum was Geraldine Carlyle Steele, whose father had chaired the board of the museum and who had lived in the cottage at one point. Many years after the theft, true, but it was possible the paintings had been stashed somewhere else in the intervening years.

She really didn't think Geraldine or Sheriff Steele could have been responsible for hiding the paintings in the cottage, but that didn't mean Geraldine's father, Montgomery Carlyle, hadn't been involved. Surely he'd been in the cottage at some point during the year and a half Geraldine and Colin had lived there. Was there anything more she could learn about him?

Hannah researched Carlyle and found a number of articles that referenced his donations to auctions, charity golf tournaments he'd competed in, and business deals he'd made. She also found a couple of articles mentioning financial trouble at the Carlyle fund. *The Wall Street Journal* had covered a bad earnings report for the third quarter in a row, noting that investors were beginning to pull their money out of the fund. The article had been published in November 1989, two months before the art heist. Hannah found a follow-up article, published six months later, about how the company had reported its best quarter in years.

She sat back and considered the information. Montgomery Carlyle's company had been in financial trouble around the time the paintings were stolen. The company had gone on to have its best quarter ever a few months later. If those facts had any connection to the theft of the paintings she couldn't see it. Even if Montgomery had somehow been involved in the theft of the paintings, how would that have helped his company? He'd not only need a way to sell the stolen paintings, but he would also have had to put the money into the company's revenue stream in a way the IRS wouldn't flag.

But that was the kind of thing the Mafia did, wasn't it?

Hannah was making a lot of assumptions. Spinning stories out of bare facts without knowing all of the details. All she knew was that Montgomery was on the museum board and that his company had been in financial trouble at the time of the theft and had recovered quickly after that. Maybe there was a connection, or maybe there wasn't. The timing could be completely coincidental. She needed to keep looking.

She found a social media page for Montgomery. It hadn't been updated in many years, obviously, since he'd passed, but the page was still active. She poked around, looking at the posts. There were plenty of golfing photos. He had also posted many pictures with friends on trips overseas or eating at fancy restaurants.

There was one man who seemed to show up in a lot of the photos, so Hannah clicked on his profile. Dickie McAllister, apparently. The top post on his page was an obituary. So Dickie, too, was gone. But his legacy page still contained plenty of information. He and Montgomery had played golf together, taken trips together, and... apparently grown up together. Dickie had posted a photo of the two of them as children. According to the post, they had been best men at each other's weddings. Hannah clicked around on Dickie's page and discovered that he had two children and five grandchildren, and that he'd been an art dealer in New York.

Now that was interesting. She clicked over to the main search page and typed in the name *Dickie McAllister*. An article in *New York Magazine* from 1991 bore the headline, Is DICKIE MCALLISTER THE ART WORLD'S WUNDERKIND?

The article went on to explore some major artists Dickie had discovered, whose work he sold for high-dollar amounts. Evidently, he'd been sought after by all the big galleries, and had risen from obscurity into the position of an art world tastemaker seemingly overnight.

So Montgomery Carlyle's best friend had a meteoric rise in the New York art world right about the time the paintings had gone missing from the art museum where Montgomery was the board chair.

It could be a coincidence.

But it sure didn't look good.

Chapter Ten

When Hannah reached Lacy's house that evening, the farm was bathed in a golden glow. The dogwood and redbud trees around the house were heavy with fresh green leaves, and the garden at the side of the house was filled with new-sprouted seedlings. Neil was leading one of their horses, Misty, into the barn, and Hannah waved as she parked next to Christine's car and stepped out.

"Hi, Hannah," Neil called to her. "Go on in. I'll be there in just a moment."

"See you then." Hannah picked up the key lime pie from her front seat and walked toward the side door that led to the kitchen. As she got closer to the house, she could hear the soft clucks of the hens in their pen. She rapped on the door, and a moment later Christine opened it and ushered Hannah inside.

"That looks amazing," Christine said. "Come on in." She took the pie to the counter, then poured Hannah a glass of lemonade.

It was nice to see Lacy's mom in the farm kitchen. Hannah had spent so much time here while she and Lacy were growing up, and she had eaten so many of Christine's chocolate chip cookies fresh out of the oven. Since moving out, Christine had been very conscious of letting Lacy make the farmhouse her home, but there was still something comforting to Hannah about seeing Christine in this kitchen once again.

"Thank you for having me," Hannah said as she took the glass. "It smells delicious in here."

"The chicken is almost done," Lacy said. She bent over and peered into the oven. "Another minute or two."

"So," Christine said, leaning against the counter. "I heard Daniel and Lori Berthold are in town. How's that going?"

"It's okay," Hannah said.

She didn't really want to go into it, so she was grateful when Christine continued without pressing. "Lori is so sweet, isn't she? She and I spent a lot of time together when they lived here. And Daniel is nice too, though not as easy to talk to."

"Really?" Hannah asked. She felt a wave of relief flood through her at the words. Maybe it wasn't just her.

"I mean, he's nice enough. He means well, and he's really kind. I've always found him a bit awkward, though. I always feel as if I'm saying the wrong thing to him, or maybe he doesn't know how to respond to what I say. Frank got along with him well, though truthfully I think it was because they didn't really speak. They were both better at silence than talking anyway."

Hannah was comforted by Christine's statement, though she didn't want to come out and say so. She was trying to figure out how to respond when the door opened and Neil came in. He took off his boots and said, "That chicken smells incredible."

"Any news on the cottage?" Lacy asked as she pulled it out of the oven.

"Colin told me today they're hoping we can get back in and start work again soon," Neil said. "He didn't give me a time frame, but he understood about *our* time frame and why we're anxious to get to work. He just wants to make sure there aren't any important clues they've missed before we start tearing down more walls."

Christine and Hannah set the table while Neil washed up, and a few minutes later, they were all seated and dishing out baked chicken and rice, buttered baby potatoes, and a fresh green salad.

As soon as Neil said grace, Lacy turned to her mom. "So, about Uncle Al. The security guard who was accused of helping in the theft. What's the story?"

Christine grimaced. "I should have said something yesterday, and I see why you're upset that I didn't." She set her napkin in her lap and took a deep breath. "The thing is, I was trying to make sense of it, and I didn't want to say the wrong thing. I guess I needed time to think about it. About whether..." Her voice trailed off.

"About whether Dad knew the paintings were in the cottage?" Lacy finished for her.

Christine nodded. "My first thought was that of course he didn't. He couldn't have. But I know how it looks that the paintings turned up in the cottage. Once you learn about Albert and that he's Frank's cousin, it's pretty hard to not make that assumption. Even so, I'm still convinced that if Albert was involved, your father didn't know."

"Why are you so sure?" Lacy asked.

Christine lifted her chin. "Because I knew Frank. He was honest as the day is long. If he'd known the art was hidden in the cottage, he would have reported it, no matter who was involved. I didn't mention that your father was related to the security guard because I couldn't bear people making rotten assumptions about your dad."

"I believe that he didn't know," Hannah said. "But is there any way to prove it?"

"I can't think of one," Christine said, misery lacing her tone. "I guess that's why I wanted to talk to you all. The police called today. They want to talk to me, which makes sense. They're coming over tomorrow."

"So you realized you couldn't avoid answering my questions about this forever?" Lacy grinned.

"More like I figured you deserved to hear it from me first," Christine said.

"You were a bit late on that one," Lacy pointed out.

"What I mean is that I wanted to tell you what I remember because you know as well as I do that your father was not involved in this. I know it looks suspicious that the art was found here, but I am certain that your father didn't know about it," Christine said. "He had no connection to it and no idea whatsoever it was here. And I hope maybe you can help me prove that."

"How would we do that?" Hannah asked.

"I suppose by figuring out who was actually involved," Christine said.

Hannah nodded. She was already hoping to do that anyway. If she could clear Lacy's father of suspicion as well, all the better. "Could you tell us a bit more about Albert? What was he like? Were the cousins close?"

"I wouldn't say they were close, exactly," Christine said. "Frank was older than Albert by ten years or so, I think. But they were cousins, so they were close in the way where that kind of age difference doesn't really matter. They were still thick as thieves when they were growing up."

Hannah nodded. Maeve and Ryder would always occupy a special place in her heart too, though they were closer in age than Frank and Albert.

"So when did Albert move to Frankfort?" Hannah asked.

"For college," Christine said. "He went to Kentucky State to major in business. I remember when he started working for the museum, actually. It was a friend who got him the job, someone who worked the night shift and said it was easy money, and you know how college kids are up all night anyway. He was talking about how excited he was to start when he came home for Christmas. But then, of course, the theft happened, and he was named as a suspect and lost the position, and the whole thing derailed his college career as well. Having his name dragged through the mud like that—well, he started having problems after."

"Problems?"

"Drinking too much, mostly. Which led to trouble holding down a job. Of course, it was hard enough to get a job in the first place for him, what with everyone thinking he was a thief, so there were some rough years in there."

"That's awful," Hannah said.

Christine took a sip of her water. "Albert had gotten into some trouble before that. I don't know all the details. I overheard some talk about him not hanging out with the best crowd, and how his grades were slipping, that kind of thing. But after the theft is when the real trouble started."

"Being held at gunpoint would be traumatic," Neil said. "Seems like he might have been suffering from PTSD."

"Could be," Christine said. "But now I wonder if that's actually what it was."

"You mean, you're wondering now if it was guilt," Hannah said quietly.

"Or something like it," Christine said. "If Albert was involved, maybe he felt bad for it. Or maybe he was forced to be involved for some reason."

"Like blackmail?" Lacy said.

"I don't know," Christine said. "I'm trying to come up with ideas. If he *was* blackmailed into letting those guards into the museum somehow, then whatever they had on him would probably eat at him, in addition to the guilt for helping with the theft. It's probably not true, but I have to wonder if it's possible."

"It would have to be some situation like blackmail where he didn't end up with the paintings, right?" Hannah said. "Because if he stole the paintings, he wouldn't have needed to get another job."

"I don't know how we'd confirm it at this point, so let's focus on what we can," Neil said, wiping his mouth with his napkin. "The real question is whether Albert ever came to the farm after the theft. Did he have the opportunity to plant those paintings in the cottage?"

"Sure," Christine said. "He came to the farm for holidays. All the big family meals happened here in the farmhouse. While we were still living in the cottage, and even after we moved into the main house, he came to the farm. But I don't know whether he was ever at the cottage. I don't remember him coming to visit us while Frank and I were still living there, but that doesn't mean he didn't."

"But even if Albert didn't come to the cottage itself..." Hannah let her voice trail off, uncertain how to finish this sentence.

"Theoretically he could have given the pictures to Frank at some point," Christine said, finishing her sentence. "Technically, yes."

"But actually, no," Lacy said. "Like you already said, Mom, there's no way Dad was involved with this."

"I know he wasn't," Hannah said. "But unfortunately he will stay under a cloud of suspicion unless we can somehow prove that Albert was an innocent victim in all this."

"As long as there is suspicion around him, there will be suspicion about Frank, now that we know where two of the paintings ended up," Christine added.

"So how do we prove that Frank knew nothing about them?" Neil asked.

"Albert's been gone for at least ten years now," Lacy said. "So he can't help us."

Christine sighed. "I've been trying to figure that out, and the only thing I can think of is reaching out to Janice."

"His ex-wife?" Lacy asked. "Quiet, with big glasses and a lot of cats?"

"She wasn't that quiet," Christine corrected. "I think she found us all overwhelming. And plenty of people like cats. Anyway, I haven't spoken to her in years. She and Albert divorced a long time ago. And she wasn't married to him at the time of the museum theft, but it's possible he said something to her about it later."

"Do you have her number?" Lacy asked.

"I have a very old number," Christine said. "It's the landline to the house they lived in over twenty years ago, and since they moved out after the divorce, I doubt it will still work."

"But you haven't tried it?" Neil said.

"No." Christine pulled a piece of paper out of her pocket and set it on the table. "I made some notes and wrote out the last phone number I had for her, just in case. But someone else has to call her. I wouldn't know what to say."

Lacy grabbed the paper and dialed the number. Hannah could hear the automated message that said the number was not in service.

"Nope," Lacy said. "But that's okay. I bet Hannah can find her."

"I can try," Hannah said. "What's her last name?"

"Her maiden name was Weissman, and then she was Johnston. She remarried at some point, but I can't remember her new name. Something with an *M*, I think. Morrow? Morrell? Something like that."

Hannah was glad she'd thought to bring her notes for the case thus far. She retrieved them from her purse now, along with a pen. "And she lived in Frankfort?"

"She did, at least when she was married to Albert," Christine said. "I don't know after that."

"Glasses, cats, quiet, and an *M* in her last name. You've got plenty to go on," Neil joked.

Hannah laughed.

He was right that it wasn't a lot to work with. But if Janice was still out there, Hannah would find her.

"What's this other stuff?" Lacy asked, tapping the page from her mom.

"That's the list of people who lived in the cabin over the years," Christine said. "Or as many as I could remember."

Lacy picked up the paper and started reading.

"'Frank and I, 1986 to January 1990,'" Lacy read from the paper. "Okay, we knew that. You moved into the main house before I was born. Then we have George Fowler, April to March 1991. That's the retired train engineer?"

"That's right. Such a nice man."

"But you said he passed away," Hannah said. "So we can't exactly talk to him."

"And then you've got Owen and Nicole Daniels from January 1991 to mid-1992. That's the couple who planted the garden, right? You said she liked bugs."

"That's right. I had to look through some old files to find their names, but that's them. Owen and Nicole."

"Anything suspicious about them?" Lacy asked.

"Well, the insect thing kind of weirded me out," Christine said. "She had a whole collection of beetles pinned to a board, and another of moths. She thought they were beautiful."

"But was there anything suspicious?" Neil asked. "Anything that might lead you to suspect they had any tie to art, the museum, or organized crime?"

"Not that I can think of," Christine said.

"Okay, we'll try to track them down. Let's see." Lacy narrowed her eyes at the page. "Joanie Gardner was your childhood friend, right?"

"That's right. I honestly can't remember exactly when she came to stay, but it was probably either before or after George Fowler. She's an old friend of mine from Louisville, and she was going through a divorce and needed a place to stay for a bit."

"Anything suspicious about her?"

"Joanie?" Christine laughed. "No. She was a school librarian."

The way she said it, it was as if school librarians were exempt from any kind of suspicion. Which Hannah couldn't totally argue with. Who ever heard of an evil school librarian?

"What's her story?" Lacy asked.

"Her dad was a contractor, and he worked a lot. He always had construction stuff lying around the house, which was so fun to a kid."

"Construction stuff?" Hannah asked.

"Oh, you know, random two-by-fours, hammers, that kind of thing. He let us pound nails in sometimes, or play with his screwdrivers."

"So you're saying Joanie knew her way around tools?" Hannah asked, raising an eyebrow.

"I mean, I guess. She worked for him for a few summers, actually. But if you're asking if she broke into the cottage and stole those tools, I don't think so. Why would she come all the way out here for a table saw? Like I said, she could pound in a nail, but so can I, and I didn't take those tools. She's a *librarian*."

"We have to suspect everyone until we clear them," Lacy said. "How can we get in touch with her?"

"I don't know," Christine said.

"Where did she go after she moved out of the cottage?" Hannah asked.

"She left a forwarding address in Louisville, but the first letter I wrote her was returned as undeliverable. I didn't know how to get ahold of her after that. We lost touch." Christine grinned at their disbelief. "You guys have to understand—in the early nineties, people didn't have cell phones or email addresses. They had physical addresses and phones that were wired to the wall in those houses. If you moved, and you didn't let people know your new address or the phone number in your new house, they couldn't get ahold of you."

"It sounds so barbaric," Lacy said, chuckling. "I don't understand how you're still in touch with anyone from back then."

"It was basically the Middle Ages," Christine said, rolling her eyes good-naturedly. "But somehow we made it out."

"Maybe she'll turn up in an online search," Hannah said. "There has to be a record of her somewhere."

"Actually, maybe—" Christine started, and then broke off. "There's probably no way they're still there, though."

"What?" Lacy said.

"Well, like I was saying, back in the day, we didn't have cell phones, which meant that if you wanted to call someone, you needed to know their actual phone number," Christine said. "So you memorized numbers or wrote them down. I've forgotten a lot of things, but one thing I'll never forget is the phone number of my childhood best friend. That's etched in there for all time. I doubt her parents still live in that house—"

"And would they still have a landline, even if they do?" Lacy asked. "Who has a landline these days?"

"A lot of people do," Christine said. "Especially if they've had it for decades. You could try calling it and see what happens."

"Sure. What is it?"

Christine rattled off the number, and Hannah wrote it down on her napkin.

"Half the time you can't remember what you had for breakfast, but you know a phone number from fifty years ago?" Lacy shook her head.

"I'm telling you, childhood phone numbers never leave. That and the lyrics to all the songs on TV when you were a child."

"I'm sorry for that. Anyway." Lacy went back to her list. "We also have someone named Mark Hillyer in 2003. Who's that?"

"A friend of your father's from college. He lost his job and needed a place to stay for a bit while he got on his feet. I think he stayed three months or so."

"I have no recollection of him at all."

"You were in your early teens. You were pretty much oblivious to anything that wasn't about you."

"I want to be offended by that, except that I know you're right," Lacy said. "We also have Colin and Geraldine Steele from 2006 to 2008, and then the last on the list is the Prentiss family in 2008, who stayed for maybe six months after Ryder burned down their house."

"Technically he only burned down the kitchen, not the whole house, as he would no doubt want us to be clear about," Hannah said.

"But we know they had nothing to do with it," Lacy said.

"Of course," Hannah said. "Aside from them, we need to look at everyone who had access to the cottage, even years later. Someone could have kept the stolen paintings somewhere—a storage unit, a safe, whatever—for years, but then could have seen an opportunity to unload them in a place they thought no one would ever look. So we need to check into everyone who had access to the space. Someone like this Mark Hillyer guy."

"So where does this get us?" Neil asked.

"I guess we try to get in touch with the people on this list we haven't spoken to yet," Hannah said.

"At least, the ones who are still alive," Neil added.

"So that's Owen and Nicole, Joanie the librarian, Colin and Geraldine Steele, and Mark Hillyer, Dad's friend," Lacy said.

"And we will also try to contact Janice M., née Johnston, née Weissman, to see if she can tell us anything about Albert."

"That's quite a list," Neil said.

Lacy shrugged. "We'll find them. And we'll figure out what happened."

She said it with such confidence that Hannah could only hope she was right.

Chapter Eleven

Monday dawned bright and clear, and Hannah tried to be happy, though a small part of her wished it was pouring rain. It wasn't that she didn't like hiking. Hiking was just walking, but out in nature, and who didn't like nature? And she probably should be excited to spend some time with her future in-laws doing something they loved.

It was just that she felt nervous about how the day would go. Would they have anything to talk about? What if it was awkward again? What if she couldn't keep up, or Daniel wanted to take her into a cave without knowing she hated them, or—

She was getting worked up, imagining things that might not take place. She was young and healthy, and she could keep up with Liam's parents. For now, she rolled over, pushed herself out of bed, and started a pot of coffee. She often spent a good chunk of her Mondays catching up on chores. That was probably what she should do this morning—laundry, clean the bathroom—but her mind was racing. Instead, she decided to use this time to see if she could find anything of interest about the names that had come up yesterday.

But first, she would settle herself the best way she knew how. As soon as her coffee was ready, she poured herself a big cup and settled in with her Bible and a notebook and looked at the passage from Isaiah again. *The wolf will live with the lamb...*

It was hard to imagine a scene like that playing out today, when it seemed like people got worked up over every difference of opinion. It was sometimes difficult to believe there would ever be a time when enemies—let alone people who merely didn't see eye to eye on every issue—could put their differences behind them and get along, maybe even learn to love one another.

That was what the Hicks painting showed, though, and it was a beautiful representation of what could happen when peace and love reigned.

She closed her Bible and pulled out the paper where she'd recorded notes at last night's dinner. Opening her laptop, her fingers hovered over the keys.

The first person Hannah wanted to look into was Janice, Albert Johnston's wife. She ran a search for *Janice Weissman*, the woman's maiden name. A social media profile for *Janice Weissman Morrow* popped up. Could it really be this easy? She clicked on the link and was taken to a page that mostly featured pictures of two small children and an adorable Pomeranian. Janice Morrow lived in Frankfort, Kentucky, and had a grown daughter and two grandchildren. There was no mention of her ex-husband, but why would there be?

Hannah clicked on a link that would allow her to send a message to Janice, and she typed it out carefully.

Hi, Janice, I'm a friend of Christine Johnston. I live in Blackberry Valley, and Christine's daughter Lacy has been my best friend since we were children. I was hoping I might be able to ask you a few questions about Albert Johnston. If you'd be willing to speak with me, I would be very grateful.

She sent the note and sat back. Hopefully Janice would receive it. Not everyone read messages that came through social media, especially from people they didn't know, but she would hope for the best.

Then she decided to go through the people who had lived in the cottage in order—or at least as close to order as Christine had been able to reconstruct. The first tenants were Christine and Frank, but Hannah didn't need to look into them when she had more promising leads.

The widower George Fowler was next, but Christine said that he passed many years ago, and a quick search turned up an obituary confirming that. He appeared to have been a nice man who loved bird-watching, model trains, and books, and was survived by two children and five grandchildren. She supposed she could try reaching out to the children and grandchildren to see if they knew anything about the paintings—and maybe she would if she didn't find anything else—but George didn't seem the most likely suspect to her.

On to Joanie Gardner. She dialed the number of Joanie's childhood landline, expecting another signal saying the number was no longer in service, but the call went through, and someone picked up.

"Hello?" It was an older woman, judging by the voice.

"Hi," Hannah replied. "My name is Hannah Prentiss, and I'm trying to get in touch with Joanie Gardner."

"Joanie's my daughter, but she hasn't lived here in decades," the woman said. "My name is Ruth. Can I ask why you're calling?"

"Christine Knicely Johnston gave me this number. She was friends with Joanie when they were children, and I was hoping to ask Joanie about a visit she made to Blackberry Valley many years ago."

"Christine Knicely?" Ruth said. "My goodness, I haven't heard that name in so long. How is Christine? Is she doing all right?"

"She's doing great," Hannah said. "She's still in Blackberry Valley. She has a daughter and will soon have a grandchild."

"That's wonderful," Ruth said. "She was always such a nice girl. And how do you know her?"

"Christine's daughter, Lacy, is my best friend," Hannah said. "Christine wasn't sure how to get in touch with Joanie, but she remembered this number and was hoping you might still live in the same house."

"Still here," Ruth said. "Going on fifty years. The kids keep trying to get us to move into a smaller place, but this is home."

"I wouldn't want to leave my home either," Hannah said. "And I'm glad you're still there, because I'd really love to find a way to get in contact with Joanie, if that's possible. Her name isn't Gardner anymore, is it?"

"She goes by White now," Ruth said. "And she's over in Lexington these days."

Hannah scribbled these facts down. "Would you be able to give me her number? I'd love to get in touch with her."

"How about this?" Ruth replied. "Why don't you give me your name and number, and I can pass it along to Joanie so she can call you if she wants to? Joanie is very particular about her privacy."

"That would be great." Hannah had been hoping she'd just pass along Joanie's number, but she supposed this was probably safer for Joanie. It was smart not to hand out someone else's contact information, especially to a complete stranger. Hannah gave the woman her number, agreed to give Ruth's best wishes to Christine, and they hung up.

She hoped Joanie would call. And if she didn't, Hannah would see if she could find her now that she had her last name and location.

She searched *Joanie White Lexington*, but still nothing looked right. There were lots of entries for the last name White, and several Joanies, but nothing that combined all the things Hannah was searching for. Was Joanie search proof? How was that possible? Her mom had said she liked privacy, but this was next level.

Hannah kept trying for a few more minutes, but she didn't turn up anything. She would have to get going soon, and she still had two sets of tenants to look into if she wanted a full picture of what she was dealing with.

She moved on to Owen and Nicole Daniels. Searching both names, she found that Nicole was an entomologist at Western Kentucky University, which explained her fascination with insects. According to the website, Nicole was still working at the university and her email was listed on the site. Hannah immediately sent a message asking if she had a few moments to chat about the cottage she'd rented in Blackberry Valley in the early nineties, hoping for the best. She had no idea if a busy professor would respond to an unsolicited and undeniably strange request. She would have to wait and see what happened.

On to Mark Hillyer, Frank's friend who'd stayed in the cottage after losing his job. An obituary popped up right away. Mark had passed last year in Des Moines, Iowa, and was survived by three kids. Like with George Fowler, Hannah would try tracking down the kids if none of the other leads panned out.

But for now, she needed to get moving if she was going to meet Liam and his parents for their hike.

Chapter Twelve

Hannah listened to the next episode of the *A Brush with Danger* podcast while she got ready to go, and packed lunches for the group to eat on the hike. In this episode, the host talked about the history of the museum. Then she interviewed a former employee of the museum, who mentioned that, despite a large endowment, the museum had been in financial trouble by the late 1980s. The former employee speculated that there might have been some financial incentive for the museum to make some of the paintings disappear.

"They were very well insured," said the employee, who remained anonymous on the podcast. It wasn't totally clear what the employee had done at the museum, but he intimated that it had to do with fundraising. "*Very* well insured."

Well, that was an interesting theory, but one she didn't have time to dwell on right now.

Liam picked Hannah up right on time, and she slid into the back seat of his Jeep next to Daniel. Lori was in the front seat. Soft bluegrass music played on the radio.

"Good morning!" Lori said, twisting around to smile at Hannah. "It's great to see you again. Are you ready for some hiking?"

"I'm looking forward to it," Hannah said, and she realized this was mostly true. Hiking might not have been her first choice of activity, but she always enjoyed being with Liam.

"We stopped at Sweet Caroline's on the way," Liam said as he handed a bag and a paper cup of coffee to her.

"Bless you." She set the coffee in a cupholder and pulled a chocolate glazed doughnut out of the bag. "This right here is why I'm marrying you." She took a bite of the doughnut and grinned.

"Chocolate glazed was always my favorite," Lori said. "We can't have doughnuts very often anymore, sadly. The doctor doesn't like it, but I miss them."

Wait, Liam's parents didn't eat doughnuts? Well, now she felt terrible eating this one. She swallowed her bite and set the doughnut on a napkin.

"Is there anything here you can eat?" She reached for the bag.

"Oh yes, we have these whole grain muffins I brought with us." Lori held up what looked like a plain brown square. "They're not as good as doughnuts but the doctor says they're better for us."

"Taste like dirt," Daniel said, his voice sullen.

"They're not that bad," Lori told him. "He just loves doughnuts," she said to Hannah.

"I don't see how one every once in a while could hurt," Daniel said. He looked at Hannah, as if he hoped she would agree with him. And in theory she did. But she also didn't know his medical history or his situation.

One thing she did know, though, was that the last thing she wanted was to side with one of the Bertholds against the other.

"I don't have to eat this, if it's a problem," Hannah said.

"Now don't be silly," Lori said. "You're young and fit. Enjoy."

Hannah didn't know what to say. They were both fitter than she was. Suddenly, the doughnut didn't taste as good.

"I'm enjoying this maple glazed," Liam said, and took a big bite from the doughnut he picked up from the console. He was trying to make things less awkward.

"As you should," Lori said, and then she began to talk about their dinner with the Dawsons the night before. "They have the cutest little dog, Josie, who's a miniature Corgi. She has the stubbiest little legs. And we had the most delicious roasted carrots with honey and a little bit of spice. I didn't know carrots could taste that good. Do you like to cook with carrots?"

Hannah realized the last part was directed at her, and she answered that she did use carrots sometimes, and Lori chattered away about the meal and something the Dawsons' grandchild was up to, and soon enough they were pulling into a parking space at the lot near the trailhead at the nature preserve. Hannah climbed out and put on the backpack she'd brought along, which held a bottle of water and sunscreen, among other things.

"You don't have hiking boots?" Daniel asked as he came around the side of the car.

She looked at her athletic sneakers. She didn't want to say she didn't hike enough to need boots. "These have always been fine for me."

"There's no ankle support," Daniel said. "And this trail can be tricky."

Hannah wasn't sure what to say, but noticed for the first time that Lori and Daniel were both wearing professional-level hiking boots. Had they brought those in their suitcases from Florida? How serious were these people about hiking?

"Hannah's always done great in her sneakers. We've been on plenty of hikes together." Liam came up beside her and took her hand.

He had hiking boots too, she now realized. His words notwithstanding, was she supposed to have bought hiking boots? Why hadn't Liam said so? He knew she didn't own any.

Liam started walking toward the edge of the parking lot, where the trail started. "Ready?"

"I love this trail," Lori said as they stepped off the pavement and onto a wide dirt path. There was a big sign with a trail map up ahead, then the trail narrowed and began a steep section of switchbacks as it climbed up the hill. "I've missed it since we left. There's nothing like this where we live now. It's all flat, flat, flat."

"I've missed this too," Daniel said. They started up the steep ascent. "You must love hiking around here, right, Hannah? Best hiking in the world."

"I do enjoy it," Hannah said. "I don't hike as much as some people, but I do like being out in nature."

"Oh, me too. I adore camping," Lori said. "Do you camp too? There's nothing like waking up surrounded by God's creation, is there? Just the sky and the trees and the birds and the Holy Spirit. It's my favorite."

"I don't do much camping," Hannah admitted. And even that was an exaggeration. By *much* she meant *any*. "My family was never really into it, so I didn't grow up doing it."

"Well, it's not too late," Daniel said. "Liam has lots of camping equipment. We used to camp every summer. A few times, we went out on weeklong backpacking trips so far out from civilization you couldn't get a cell signal."

"My favorite was the one with the inflatable canoe," Lori said. "Remember that time we flipped the canoe and all our stuff went floating down the river?"

"Packs, tents, food—all of it, gone," Daniel said. "And the satellite phone and my car keys were in my pack, so we were really and truly in trouble."

"Dad tried to swim after it and almost got taken out by a log," Liam said, laughing.

"I thought we were goners." Lori chuckled. "I don't know what we would have done if those men hadn't seen our stuff floating by on the river and scooped it all up in their motorboat."

"They came motoring up the river and asked if it belonged to us. They had the packs and even the canoe piled in their boat," Liam said. "They thought we were goners too."

"Oh goodness, that was such a great trip," Lori said, shaking her head.

Hannah bit her lip. That was their idea of a good vacation? It sounded terrible. They'd almost died. Why would anyone want to do that?

"But that wasn't as bad as some of the scrapes we got into while caving," Daniel said. "Now, we had some real messes there."

Liam was an experienced caver and trained in cave rescues, so she supposed she shouldn't be surprised he'd gotten it from his dad.

Why was this hill so steep? Was she the only one who was getting winded? It wasn't like she'd never been hiking before. Just last month she'd hiked as she led the *Destination Discovery* team to some caves, but that trail was much less steep than this one.

"We don't need to tell her about those, Dad," Liam said. "Or she'll never let me go caving again."

"You're not going to go with him?" Daniel said, looking at Hannah.

"She has before, but Hannah doesn't like caves." Liam laughed.

"You don't like caves?" Daniel's voice rose. "How could you not like caves?"

What was she supposed to say? That she didn't like dark, small, dangerous holes in the ground filled with creepy-crawly things? "I'm kind of claustrophobic, so they're not my favorite."

"I took Hannah into the cave at the state park last fall," Liam said. "And she did great."

"And I'm totally fine with Liam going caving," Hannah said. "It's something he loves, and I would never want to take that away from him. It's just not really my thing."

"I've never liked caving much myself," Lori said. "I told Daniel early on I'd rather not go that far underground, and for the most part he was okay with that." She turned her head and gave Hannah a smile.

"You're missing out, is all," Daniel said. "Some of the most gorgeous things I've ever seen have been in caves."

"Hannah doesn't have to go caving with me," Liam said. "It's totally fine that there are things she likes and things she doesn't. Her interests don't have to line up perfectly with mine." He winked at Hannah, who smiled back.

But Daniel made a noise at the back of his throat that Hannah couldn't interpret. "What about skiing? Do you like that?"

Skiing wasn't a big thing in western Kentucky. If one were willing to drive several hours, it was doable. But it wasn't something her family had ever been into.

"I tried it once in college," Hannah said. She swiped her arm across her face as she made the turn for another switchback. "With some friends who didn't bother to explain that you don't just point your skis downhill and go."

"They didn't show you how to control your skis or how to slow down?" Lori asked.

"Not a word. It didn't go well." She had never in her life tumbled head over heels so many times in the space of an hour. There had been snow inside her jacket, her boots, and every other article of clothing.

"I should say not," Lori said.

"So you don't ski?" Daniel sounded affronted. "Liam skis expert hills with his eyes closed. Moguls, slaloms, you name it. He's been skiing since he could walk."

Of course he had. Liam was athletic and strong and fearless. Plus, he'd been doing it since before he knew better.

"I think it's one of those things you really have to learn when you're a kid," Hannah said. She stepped on a slab of rock and it shifted a bit beneath her feet, but she caught her balance quickly. Liam reached out to steady her anyway, before they moved on.

"Lots of adults learn to ski," Daniel said. "Lori did."

"I don't ski well," Lori said. "I'm just trying to keep up with these guys. I'll never be able to do the kinds of runs they can."

"Hannah doesn't have to ski if she doesn't want to either," Liam said, with a finality in his voice that couldn't be missed. "She doesn't have to do the things I do or like the things I like. She is good at and enjoys all kinds of things herself."

Again, Daniel made a noise that Hannah didn't understand, but Lori spoke up. "We'd love to know more about that. What do you like to do in your free time, Hannah?"

Hannah thought for a moment. "I love to cook, obviously."

"That's work," Daniel said.

"Not when I do it for myself or my loved ones," Hannah said. "I also love to read, and I love to visit museums. I love coffee and catching up with my friends. My best friend, Lacy, hosts a monthly puzzle night, and I've grown to like puzzles because of that. I love the beach. That's probably what I miss most about living in Los Angeles, actually. Not the weather, but access to the beach. There's something about the ocean that soothes my soul."

"I love the beach too," Lori said. "The sound of the waves, the smell of the salty air, and the feel of the sand. It's heaven on earth."

"Do you surf?" Daniel perked up, apparently at the idea that she might love some high-action, high-danger sport after all.

"No." Hannah had dated a few surfers over the years, but she figured she didn't need to say that now. "I like to bodyboard and bodysurf. That's enough for me. And I like to sit with a book and enjoy the sunshine."

She felt like she was giving the wrong answer once again. Lori was trying to help, and Hannah appreciated that, but she felt like no matter what she said, even when she was talking about things she loved, it wasn't good enough for Daniel.

"I'll take you to the beach someday." Liam hung back and waited until she caught up with him on the trail. "We'll go to the beach and sit in our chairs and read books and stare at the water for as long as you like."

Hannah had never loved him more. She was grateful to him, and knew that it was Liam she was marrying and not his dad. Liam loved her and supported her. He didn't care that she didn't like caving or skiing and camping. It was what Liam thought that mattered.

But it still felt like this was going to be a very long hike.

Chapter Thirteen

The view from the top of the hill was, as promised, gorgeous. As they ate the turkey and avocado sandwiches with garlic aioli Hannah had packed—she'd been inspired by the sandwich Lacy had bought her—Hannah had to admit she didn't mind this part of hiking.

It was getting up here that was hard, and she was surprised to find that the trip down wasn't actually much easier. Lori and Daniel went ahead while Liam stayed with Hannah, carefully picking their way over the rocks and roots on the steep trail. By the time they made it back to the car, Lori and Daniel were eating grapes and cheese on a picnic blanket and looking rested and refreshed.

"Well, that was fun," Lori said cheerfully. "Thank you for coming with us, Hannah."

"I enjoyed it," Hannah said, and it was true.

Lori chattered happily about her favorite hikes they'd done—including Half Dome in Yosemite and South Kaibab in the Grand Canyon, two of the hardest hikes in the country—until they got back to Blackberry Valley, where Liam dropped his parents off at his place. It was still early afternoon, and Liam told his parents that he and Hannah were going to grab some coffee.

"And by coffee I mean ice cream," Liam whispered as soon as his parents were out of earshot.

"Have I ever mentioned I love you?" Hannah laughed.

"You could always say it again."

Instead, she leaned over and planted a kiss on his cheek.

A few minutes later, he had parked in front of the local ice cream shop. The small wooden building wasn't much to look at from the outside, but they served the richest, creamiest ice cream Hannah had ever had. They ordered—coconut and blueberry crunch in a cone for Liam, chocolate brownie crunch and chocolate mint chip in a cup for Hannah—and sat in the sunshine at a wooden picnic table in the yard.

"Thank you," Liam said.

"For what?" She scooped up a spoonful of ice cream, digging out a chunk of brownie.

"For coming today. I know it was a lot for you."

"It was fine. The view was nice."

"I don't really mean the hike," Liam said. "I mean, I know my dad can be a lot."

Hannah tried to think of what to say. "He's nice." It sounded flat even to her ears. She swallowed some ice cream and tried again. "But I don't think he likes me very much."

"He does like you," Liam said. "That's the thing. I know it sounded like he was grilling you today, but he doesn't mean it. I don't think he intends to sound so judgmental. Believe it or not, he's trying to connect."

"He is?" She was pretty sure Liam was only trying to make her feel better, which she appreciated, sort of. She'd prefer that he told her how to get on his dad's good side instead.

"I know it doesn't seem like it. He's looking for things you have in common, and he can't imagine a world in which people don't think like he does. He's kind of old-school that way. But it doesn't mean he doesn't like you, I promise. He told me last night that he thinks I made a great choice."

"He did?"

"Honest," Liam said. "So I know he's awkward, but believe me when I say it's him trying to connect with you, and just doing a really bad job of it."

Hannah nodded. She would try as well, though it was hard to see how a close relationship with her future father-in-law was possible.

"My mom loves you, by the way."

"Your mom is so sweet. I love her too." Hannah scooped up another bite of her ice cream. "Does she really go camping and caving and skiing just because your dad enjoys those things?"

"She likes them too," Liam said with a chuckle. "Except caving. But she did initially get into them because my dad wanted her to."

Hannah ran the spoon around the edge of her cup, scooping up the quickly melting ice cream. Would Liam make a similar request of her?

"It doesn't mean I expect you to do the same," Liam said, as if reading her mind. "You have your own likes and desires and preferences, and I'm fine with you exploring those while I explore mine. Then afterward, we can come together and talk about them, which is what I enjoy anyway."

She reached out and took his hand. "Thank you."

"I love you for who you are, Hannah, not who I could make you into. I do have a question, though. Why didn't you mention solving mysteries when you were listing things you like?"

"That's not really a hobby," Hannah said.

"You do it enough that it could almost be a part-time job."

"One job is enough, thank you very much."

He licked his cone. "Okay, then, I'll come out and ask directly. Are there any updates on those paintings?"

Hannah laughed. "Yes and no, I guess. I don't think I'm any closer to finding out how they got from the museum to the cottage. But there have been a few leads."

"Such as?"

Hannah realized she hadn't really updated him at all since she'd started trying to find answers. "There are a few theories around how the museum theft went down," Hannah said. "Including the idea that the mob was involved."

"That's not totally crazy," Liam said. "There used to be some organized crime up that way."

"Yeah, it seems that there was some evidence that a gangster named Vinnie Amelio may have been involved."

"What evidence?"

"A list of the stolen paintings was found in his possession, for one thing," Hannah said. "With their estimated values. In his handwriting."

"That seems like a pretty solid link," Liam said.

"But the cops were never able to prove anything," Hannah said. "Another theory is that it was an inside job. A former employee who was interviewed on the *A Brush with Danger* podcast suggested that the paintings might have been stolen to collect the insurance money. I've been wondering if maybe someone like Geraldine Steele's dad, who was the chair of the museum board, might have been involved.

Especially because his company was in financial trouble before the theft, and was doing great soon after."

"Whoa. There's a lot to absorb there." Liam took a bite and chewed, then said, "Who was this employee?"

"He stayed anonymous, but he worked in fundraising, I think."

"Did he offer any proof of the insurance fraud idea?"

"No. But that doesn't mean it's not true."

"Fair enough. Was the museum in financial trouble?"

"The former employee said it was." She scooped up a bite of mint chip and savored the cool sweetness accentuated with earthy chocolate. "Plus, don't arts organizations sometimes struggle to raise adequate funding?"

"That's quite an elaborate conspiracy theory." He licked his cone again. "Is there any chance it's true?"

"It's hard to say," Hannah said. "Actually, why wouldn't they sell the paintings, if they needed cash that badly? Surely works like those would earn more at auction than through insurance."

"And an institution dedicated to preserving art isn't the kind of place that would make works by ten of the most important American painters disappear from public view for cash," Liam pointed out.

"Right," Hannah said. "So that theory seems the least likely to me. But it's possible. And then there's the theory that the guard who let the thieves in that night was involved in the theft."

"But he let them in because they posed as cops, right? And then they tied him up at gunpoint."

"Yes, but the question is, was that just for show? Was he actually in on it? Did he know they weren't really cops, and go along with getting tied up so they all had a cover story? It's not clear. Which is complicated by the fact that this guard was Frank Johnston's cousin."

Liam let out a low whistle. "And then the paintings were found in a house Frank owned and lived in?"

"Yeah, it doesn't look great."

"Is there any chance Frank knew that the paintings were there?"

"No, but we need to prove that. Christine gave me a list of people who lived in the cottage over the years, and I'm looking into them. Some of them have passed away, but there are a couple I've reached out to and a couple we know, like Uncle Gordon, as well as Colin and Geraldine Steele."

"The Steeles lived there? And Geraldine's father was on the museum board?"

"It looks a bit strange, doesn't it?"

"I guess I didn't realize Geraldine's family was into art."

Hannah dug out a chunk of chocolate brownie and popped it in her mouth. "Her dad was the president of a bank or something like that. Really wealthy, blue blood, all that. And I guess he liked art."

"How did she end up marrying a small-town sheriff?"

"Colin is handsome and charming, and I'm sure he's quite a catch."

"Even so, I bet her dad wasn't happy that she fell in love with a penniless policeman. It sounds like an old-fashioned romance novel, doesn't it?"

Hannah shrugged. "She probably had enough money for both of them. Besides, he's a good man, and you can't help who you fall in love with."

"I guess."

"You think I *wanted* to fall in love with a man who rushes headlong into dangerous fires for a living?" Hannah teased. "If I'd had the choice, I would have fallen for someone with a sedate desk job so I'd never have to worry about my husband getting hurt or killed in the line of duty. But you're the one I fell in love with."

"You're underestimating desk jobs," Liam said. "You can get a nasty paper cut if you're not careful."

Hannah shook her head. "Anyway, Geraldine's father had money and connections, and he was on the board of the museum. Presumably he also knew a lot about the artwork and the museum itself. And there's the unexplained turnaround in his company's finances."

"And then the paintings turned up in a house Geraldine once lived in," Liam said.

"Yep."

"What did Colin and Geraldine say when you asked them about it?"

"I haven't talked to them," Hannah said.

"Why not?"

"Because he's the sheriff, and it's his investigation," Hannah reminded Liam. "It feels a bit silly for me to grill them when I'm not involved in an official capacity."

Liam nodded. "When you say it like that, it does seem ridiculous. But there's always another way to get what you need."

"What do you suggest in this case?" She was almost done with her ice cream, but she scraped out every last spoonful. "Wait. Is there some kind of reciprocal thing that means you'd be able to get answers out of him, since you're the fire chief and he's the sheriff?"

Liam laughed. "Sadly, no. What it usually means is that there's a fierce rivalry between us over who gets dunked the most in the dunk tank at the high school carnival, but that's as far as it goes."

"So what were you thinking?"

"You're right that you can't just waltz in and start questioning the sheriff. But he's not really the one you want to talk to anyway, is he? Geraldine is the one with the tie to the museum, right? And the one whose family knows about art and had the connections."

"I guess you're right." Hannah was starting to see what he was hinting at, and once it was out there, it seemed obvious.

"So we go talk to Geraldine."

"We can't just show up at her house and start asking questions," Hannah said, shaking her head.

"Of course not," Liam said. "But if we had a legitimate reason to go over and talk to her, it'd be a different story."

"Sure," she said. "Do you have any ideas for how we could pull that off?"

Liam popped the rest of his cone into his mouth and gave her an ear-to-ear grin. "As a matter of fact, I do."

Chapter Fourteen

The Steeles' driveway wound under towering sycamore and redbud trees, past fields where half a dozen horses grazed. The driveway curved and the house appeared—a three-story Victorian, complete with gingerbread trim and intricate moldings. It was set on a rise overlooking the horse pastures and must have had a nice view of the hills on the far side of the valley.

A small sign directed visitors to turn right when the driveway split, and they parked in front of a small building clad in weathered gray boards and big windows. Hannah wasn't sure the gallery would be open on a Monday, but when they approached, they found the door open and the lights on.

Inside the building, white walls gleamed under warm lights, and a dozen paintings decorated the space. There was no one at the desk along the rear wall, but a small sign said to ring the bell for assistance.

Liam hit the bell and then started walking toward the paintings. He stopped in front of the closest one, a picture of historic downtown Blackberry Valley at sunset. The lights in the shops were starting to come on, and the sky was lit with a fiery golden light.

A door behind the desk opened, and Geraldine walked out. Her long brown hair was pulled into a low ponytail, and she wore jeans and a loose white shirt that were both dotted with paint. She was scrubbing at a swatch of light blue paint on her hand with a paper towel as she walked toward them. Was Hannah imagining it, or did her smile falter a bit when she saw who had come to call?

"Hello," Geraldine said. "Please excuse the way I look. I've been working on a new painting in the back."

"You look great," Hannah said. Even though Geraldine was wearing what Hannah assumed were painting clothes, she somehow looked chic and put together, like an advertisement for a working artist.

"It's good to see you both, and congratulations on the engagement. I don't think I've seen either of you since I heard the good news."

"Thank you," Hannah said. "We're very happy."

"Have you picked a date?" Geraldine asked.

"Not yet," Hannah said. "We hope to figure out it out soon, though."

"So what brings you in today?" Geraldine asked.

"My parents are in town for a visit," Liam said.

"I heard they were around. Please tell them hello for me."

"I will," Liam said. "The thing is, as much as they love Florida, they also miss home. They've been talking about how much they love seeing these hills again. My mom's birthday is this Friday, and I'd like to give her a painting that reminds her of this place. A little bit of Blackberry Valley in the midst of the Florida sunshine."

"That's a lovely idea," Geraldine said.

It was a lovely idea, and so incredibly thoughtful. How could Hannah not love a man who loved his mom?

"Do you have any thoughts about what kind of painting she might like?" Geraldine asked. "Most of my pieces are from this area, but as you can see, there's a pretty big variety."

"They're beautiful," Hannah said, and it was true. There were paintings showing the hills that surrounded the town, open fields and barns, and memorable structures in the town bathed in golden light.

"They really are," Liam said. "I think what she misses most are the hills, so I think focusing there would be best."

"There are several of them on that wall," Geraldine said.

They wandered over to the wall she indicated, and Hannah's gaze immediately caught on one that showed the view from the place they'd been earlier today. Hills rolled out, one after another. Wisps of fog gathered in the far reaches of the valleys, and it was all bathed in a soft glow.

"Is this the nature preserve?" Hannah asked.

"Good eye," Geraldine said. "That one's painted from a photo I took at the top of the Sycamore Trail. Do you know it?"

"We were just there," Liam said, smiling. "I think that's the one, don't you, Hannah?"

"I think your mom will love it," Hannah said. "It will make her happy every time she sees it."

"I think so too. We'll take it."

Hannah noted the price on the small square taped to the wall next to the picture. It wasn't exorbitant, but it wasn't cheap either. She knew that Liam was careful with money in general, and if he was going to splurge on something, she was glad it was a gift for his mom.

"Wonderful. I'm so glad you like it." Geraldine smiled. "Do you want to take it now, or would you like to have it shipped to Florida?"

"I'd like to take it now and give it to her on Friday," Liam said. "We're celebrating her birthday dinner at the Hot Spot that evening. I can ship it to her later."

"If you want to bring it back after you've shown it to her, I'd be happy to ship it to her from here," Geraldine offered. "That way you know it will be packed safely."

"That would be great," Liam said.

Geraldine lifted the painting off its hook and carried it to the counter and set it down. He followed her and handed her his credit card.

While they chatted about where his mom might hang the piece, Hannah tried to figure out how to casually bring up the topic they'd come here to discuss. Nothing sounded right in her head. *Say, since you like art, did you hear about the stolen art we found in the house you used to live in?* How was she supposed to casually bring this up?

But as she was still trying to figure it out, Liam said, "We ran into Colin the other day at the cottage on Bluegrass Hollow Farm. Did you hear about the paintings we found hidden in a wall over there? How crazy was that?"

Geraldine handed him back his credit card and smiled. She didn't show any outward sign of tension or confusion, but something in her manner changed at his words. Where she had been open and warm before, she suddenly became closed off, as if a veil had fallen.

"I try not to discuss the cases my husband is involved with," she said. There was a twitch at the corner of her mouth, though she maintained her smile. "He doesn't tell me what he's working on, and if I hear of it, I try not to get involved. I'm sure you understand."

"Of course," Hannah said, both to defuse the situation, and because she could tell that Geraldine wasn't going to change her mind. The set of her jaw and the tone of her voice made it clear she wouldn't be convinced to slip up and tell them something. "We understand."

"It does make sense," Liam agreed. "Thank you for your help. My mom will love the painting."

"Of course. Just bring it here when you want it shipped," she said.

Liam carried the painting to the car and tucked it into the back, then they both climbed inside.

"She really did not want to talk about that," Hannah said as he started the engine.

"Or maybe she couldn't." Liam turned the car around. "Maybe she really isn't allowed to talk about something Colin is investigating."

"I guess so." It made some sense. The sheriff couldn't go around talking about the cases he was investigating. And it followed that his wife wouldn't be able to either.

"Or maybe she truly doesn't know."

"I don't think so. She would have said if she didn't know what we were talking about, right?"

"Maybe not. Maybe when she heard me say Colin was investigating the case, she knew she wasn't able to talk about it, but really had no idea what we were suggesting." Liam drove the car along the driveway, beneath the towering trees.

Hannah thought about it for a moment before she shook her head. "No, she knew. She knew as soon as we walked in why we were really there. Didn't you see her pause when she saw us?"

"No."

"She recovered quickly, and I only noticed because I was watching closely, but I'm certain she knew why we were there as soon as she spotted us."

Liam shrugged. "I believe you, and I guess that's why you're so good at investigating mysteries. You're good at reading people. But I totally missed it." He was quiet for a moment, and then he laughed. "It must have been a nice surprise for her when I actually bought something."

"I think it was. But it wasn't enough motivation to make her actually talk to us," Hannah said.

"Sadly, it was not." Liam turned onto the main road and headed toward town. "Well, at least I got a birthday present for my mom out of it, so it wasn't a pointless trip."

"It wasn't a pointless trip in any case. We learned something."

"What was that?"

"That Geraldine knows something," Hannah said. "Not only that, but we know that whatever it is, she very much did not want to tell us about it."

—

Chapter Fifteen

Lacy called shortly after Liam dropped Hannah off at her apartment. He had to work this evening and Hannah was looking forward to a hot shower, followed by a dinner of pasta with fresh asparagus and ricotta. But she was happy to hear from Lacy and answered the call.

"Hi," Lacy said. "How'd the hike go?"

"It went okay," Hannah said.

"Better or worse than dinner?"

"Better than dinner," Hannah said. "The hike itself was all right, but Liam's dad doesn't understand why I don't like camping or caving or skiing."

"Because you have better things to do than die in the wilderness?"

"Thank you." Lacy always somehow managed to say exactly what Hannah needed to hear. "Liam says he's just trying to connect with me."

"Then I'm sure it's true."

"I don't know."

"Why would Liam lie about that?"

"To make me feel better." It felt good to say it out loud.

"I think you're worried for no reason, Hannah. Liam loves you. So maybe his dad is awkward and doesn't know how to connect. It doesn't mean he doesn't like you."

"I suppose." But Hannah wasn't convinced.

"I have some news that will cheer you up," Lacy said.

"What's that?"

"I've been listening to the podcast about the theft, and in the fourth episode, they mentioned that the police had released the security camera footage from the Witherspoon Museum on the night of the theft."

"Oh wow. I've got to catch up." After thinking for a moment, she added, "If that footage is online, why haven't I come across it yet?"

"Probably because it was released in 1991, before the internet was really commercialized and available to the public. I mean, the World Wide Web didn't exist until that year. I don't know what they had to do back then to release footage—maybe mail physical copies of VHS tapes to news stations or something like that?"

"It truly was barbaric then, wasn't it?" Hannah joked.

"The Stone Age," Lacy agreed. "But anyway, the podcast made a digital copy and put it online. You can find the link on their website. The quality is not great, but at least you can see how it all happened."

"I'll have to check that out. Thanks for the tip."

"No problem," Lacy said. "But wait, I haven't told you the best news yet."

"What's that?"

"Sheriff Steele said they're done gathering evidence," Lacy said, her voice high with excitement. "We can go back in and start working on the cottage again tomorrow. Gus brought new tools and supplies over today to get everything set up so they can start first thing, and Neil is going to take the day off to finish demoing the kitchen."

"Are Liam and Archer back on?" Hannah asked.

"He already checked with them, and they both have to work, sadly. And we're already behind, so Neil is going to get to work. It won't be as much fun, but it'll be progress."

"I'm so glad." Hannah meant it.

"Hopefully we'll get this thing done before the baby shows up." Lacy's tone had changed from excitement to concern. "Otherwise, we'll really be in a tricky spot."

Hannah listened to the podcast while she cooked dinner and reached the episode that Lacy had mentioned, in which the host, Sarah Smalley, talked about the security camera footage. Hannah opened her laptop and went to the show's website. Sure enough, there was a link that opened a grainy black-and-white video.

The technology had really improved in the intervening thirty years, but she could still clearly see a man sitting in a small room surrounded by computer screens. The man appeared to be Albert, and the room must have been where he sat during the overnight hours to guard the museum. The camera caught him from the back, but this guy had the same curly long hair Hannah had seen in the photo in the newspaper. He was hunched over a textbook on a table, but looked up when a doorbell rang.

She watched as, in the video, Albert got up and walked out of the small guard room. The video picked up from a different camera angle, with Albert peering through a small window in a thick metal door. He pressed a button on what had to be an intercom and said something, but the footage didn't pick up the sound. After what seemed like some back and forth, he opened the door.

Two police officers—or men dressed as police officers with their hats pulled down low—appeared in the open doorway. Albert stepped aside and let them inside. As soon as the door closed, the first police officer pointed a gun at Albert.

Albert quickly held up both hands and kept them above his head while the other police officer pulled a rope out of his pocket and tied Albert's hands behind his back, then used duct tape to cover his mouth. Albert reluctantly let himself be led into the guard room.

The camera in that space picked up the shot of the two thieves shoving Albert into the room. They both turned away from the cameras, and each took something out of his pocket. They took off their police hats and replaced them with balaclavas. Now thoroughly disguised, they tied Albert's feet together and used handcuffs to chain him to the console with the computer screens. Then, the men left the guard room, leaving Albert behind.

It was unnerving to watch. The footage made it pretty clear to Hannah that Albert had no idea those men weren't police when he'd let them in. That he'd been duped, held at gunpoint, and locked up against his will.

The video went on to show shots from inside the galleries, as the two men walked through the museum, stopping occasionally to unhang a painting. They shoved some of the smaller pictures into a garbage bag that one of them must have taken from his pocket, but she watched in horror as one of the men approached a larger painting—it looked like a big flower, and Hannah guessed it was the

Georgia O'Keefe—and used a knife to cut the canvas just inside the edge of the frame. The priceless painting curled down toward the ground. The thief ripped it free of its frame, then he rolled it up and stuffed it in the bag.

The two thieves worked methodically, and it seemed pretty clear that they knew exactly which paintings they were looking for and where to find them. It was chilling, watching them work their way through the museum, taking only the most valuable pieces.

When they had finished, both men walked out of the galleries and out the door they'd entered originally, leaving Albert tied up in the guard room. The footage cut off.

Hannah wasn't sure she was glad she'd watched the footage, suspecting that the images she'd seen would stay with her for a while. But at least now she knew what had happened, and having seen it, she felt confident that Albert was innocent. A sense of relief flowed through her. This would help prove that Albert—and by extension Frank—wasn't behind the crime after all.

And yet, when she scrolled down and read the comments beneath the video, she realized that not everyone saw it that way.

Did you see the way he didn't ask the "police" for badges? It was almost as if he knew they weren't actually police.

He didn't even fight back. Was the gun even real?

Why did he open the door at all? Protocol said that he wasn't allowed to open the door for anyone, period. The only thing that makes sense is if he was in on it.

The guard saw these men without balaclavas. He absolutely saw their faces. You can see it in the video. So why is it that he cannot identify either one of them after the fact? Even when shown photos of the mobsters the police suspected of being behind the thefts, he would never identify them. Which only makes sense if he was in on it too.

The certainty Hannah had felt a moment ago evaporated as she read through the comments. Now that someone pointed it out, why *hadn't* Albert asked to see badges before opening the door to the police officers? And he *had* seen their faces. Why wasn't he able to identify them? The commenters were right that he hadn't fought back when the thieves tied him up. Was that because—as Albert had always maintained—he was afraid, since they'd pulled a gun on him? Or was this commenter right, and Albert didn't fight because he knew he wasn't in any actual danger?

Could Albert have really been in on this heist from the beginning?

Hannah sat back, more confused than ever.

She wanted to slam the lid of her laptop shut, but she didn't want to take out her frustration on the poor computer. Instead, she closed that window and opened her email to scan through it one last time. There was an invoice, an advertisement for a sale at a store she liked, someone fundraising for a cause she'd supported in the past—

And a message from Nicole Daniels. The bug lady.

> *Hannah,*
>
> *I'm happy to hear news from Blackberry Valley. Owen and I have many fond memories of our time there in that cottage. I'd be glad to talk to you about it. Would you have*

any time Wednesday morning? I live in Bowling Green these days.

Nicole

Hannah wrote back right away to confirm that Wednesday morning would work perfectly for her, and offered to come out to Bowling Green to see her. Hopefully Nicole would respond soon. In the meantime, she checked her social media and found a message from someone named Janice Morrow. Albert's ex-wife.

Hi, Hannah,

I'm glad Christine is doing well, though I'm sorry to hear about Frank's passing. And Lacy all grown up and married! She was just a little thing when I last saw her.

I don't like to talk about what happened with Albert, as those are painful memories, but I have to admit I am intrigued by the news that some of the stolen paintings have been found. I actually live not too far from Blackberry Valley these days, in Cave City. Would you be interested in coming by sometime to discuss?

Hannah typed a reply in the affirmative, and it seemed that Janice was active online at that moment because a response came almost immediately, inviting her to stop by tomorrow. They arranged a time in the morning, and Hannah said she looked forward to seeing her.

At last, she was making progress.

Maybe she'd finally find out what really happened.

Chapter Sixteen

The next morning, Hannah was on her way to pick up Lacy for their jaunt to Cave City when Lacy called her on her hands-free system.

"Someone broke in again," Lacy said without introduction. "Someone actually broke into the cottage and took Gus's tools—again!"

"What?" Hannah couldn't have heard that right. "Are you sure?"

"Positive. You know how I said we got approval to start work again this morning? Gus brought his tools over—replacements he just bought—but when Neil met him at the cottage this morning, the door was jimmied open, and the tools were gone. Again."

"Who on earth would do that?"

"I don't know, but the police are on their way over. I'm not going to be able to come with you today, Hannah. I need to stay here and deal with this," Lacy said with clear regret.

"Of course. I'm so sorry."

"I wish we knew what was going on and why this was happening. It's crazy. And the work will be delayed again," Lacy said plaintively. "I'm getting worried we won't finish it before the baby comes."

"I'm sure the police will figure it out," Hannah said, hoping Lacy couldn't tell that she was trying to convince herself as well. Then she had a thought. "What about the wire?"

"What?"

"The copper wire that wasn't taken last time. That was still in the cottage, right? Was it stolen this time?"

"I don't know. Hang on." She must have moved the phone away from her ear, because Hannah heard some muffled conversation before she came back on. "Neil says the wire is still here."

"That's odd, isn't it?"

"I guess so? I don't know. I'm sorry, Hannah. I'm not really thinking straight right now."

"That's totally understandable," Hannah said. "Go deal with that situation. I'll be fine."

"I'm sorry I can't be there with you when you talk to Albert's ex-wife, but I want to hear all about it."

"I'll keep you updated," Hannah promised. They said goodbye and ended the call.

She pulled into the next driveway and turned around, then headed toward Cave City, puzzling over this latest theft. What was going on at the cottage? It seemed strange—almost too strange to be believed—that the cottage had been broken into yet again. Either someone was *really* interested in tools, or there was something else going on.

But if it was true that the tools had been taken by someone hoping to prevent them from finding the paintings hidden in the walls, what was this theft about? The artwork had already been discovered. So why steal tools again? Was someone hoping to slow down the renovation process for some other reason?

Was there any chance the tools had been stolen because there were more secrets hidden in the cottage? What if there were more paintings? Hannah wondered how she hadn't thought of it before. Ten paintings had been stolen from the museum, and so far only three had been recovered. Were more pieces—perhaps even all seven of the ones still missing—hidden in the cottage somewhere? Was there a gold mine of important artwork behind those walls?

When the sheriff allowed them to get back in and start tearing apart the cottage, Hannah was going to look very carefully to see if anything else might still be hiding in there.

Janice's house in Cave City was a standard suburban tract home— big garage fronting the street, blue siding, porch surrounding the entrance. The door and shutters were painted a contrasting melon color, and the porch was held up with wooden posts in a nod to the modern farmhouse style. A towering old oak tree shaded the yard.

When Hannah knocked on the front door, it was opened by a woman with gray hair, big blue eyes, and dark, heavy-framed glasses. An orange-and-white cat rubbed against her legs. "Hannah?"

"Hi, Janice. It's great to meet you." Hannah held out the bag of muffins she'd brought from Sweet Caroline's Bakery. "I'm so sorry Lacy couldn't come. Something came up at home, and she wasn't able to make it after all."

"That's too bad." Janice accepted the bag. "I was looking forward to seeing her all grown up. But I'm glad to meet you. Please come in."

She led Hannah into a formal living room with antique furniture topped by doilies and lots of framed family photos. A cat tree stood in the corner, and a black-and-white cat slept on the top platform. Janice led Hannah past that room and a kitchen, then into another room with overstuffed couches and a large television, which was playing a home-shopping channel on mute. On the screen, someone held a gold chain so that it glinted in the overhead lights.

Janice sat down, picked up the remote, and turned the television off. "Excuse the mess. Bryan is traveling for work this week, and I tend to get lazy and let things slide a bit while he's gone."

Hannah saw that there were a few empty coffee mugs on the coffee table, but beyond that it didn't seem very messy to her, aside from a startling amount of cat hair. Hannah sat, and a small calico cat jumped up and settled on the other end of the couch.

"Your timing is good," Janice said. "Just an hour before I got your message, I got a call from a police officer in Blackberry Valley, wanting to talk to me about some paintings."

"I guess I'm not surprised they tracked you down," Hannah said.

"You're not working with the police yourself, right?"

"No," Hannah said. "I'm not working against them, you understand. I'm happy to share anything I learn with them. But I'm primarily here because Christine and Lacy wanted to find out more about the paintings that ended up on their property."

"Well, I told the officer who called that they're welcome to come by, but I didn't mention I was meeting with you. I wasn't sure if I should."

"It's fine with me," Hannah said. "I don't see any reason not to keep everyone on the same page."

"Good. That's what I was hoping you'd say." She opened the bag of muffins. "Now, these look delicious. This was very kind. Would you like one?"

"I ate shortly before I came here, so I'm all right," Hannah said. "Thank you for taking the time to talk with me. Especially since you don't like to discuss those days."

Janice pulled out a blueberry crumble muffin and set it on a napkin from the bag. "I don't typically like talking about them, but I will admit I am very curious to hear about these paintings you found. Albert would have given so much to have learned the truth of what happened to them, so I almost wish he were here to hear it." She paused and then laughed. "And I haven't wished I could see him since the divorce, so you know this is a big deal. You said two of the paintings were found in that cottage on the Johnston land?"

"That's right," Hannah said. "Paintings by Edward Hicks and Thomas Cole."

"Which ones were those? I'm afraid I don't know very much about art."

"I didn't know them either." Hannah pulled up the photos of the pieces on her phone. "These are the paintings." She handed Janice the device.

The older woman pulled a pair of reading glasses from her pocket and peered at the screen. "I remember these. The animal one and the hill one. Albert used to look at pictures of these—of all the stolen artwork—all the time. I always liked these. Some of the other ones just looked like a mess to me, all splatters of paint and blocks of color that I could have done. But these are pretty, aren't they?"

"They're beautiful paintings," Hannah agreed. "What do you mean, Albert used to look at pictures of the paintings?"

"Oh, he went over that night in his mind thousands of times, trying to figure out what he could have done differently. Trying to figure out where he'd gone wrong. He was haunted by it, really, and it's not all that surprising, is it? Not only was he blamed for the theft of millions of dollars' worth of art, but everyone thought he was in on it somehow."

That made sense to Hannah. It didn't help to dwell on the past, but that didn't always stop people, especially if they felt they'd made a mistake.

Janice broke off a piece of the muffin and popped it in her mouth. She chewed thoughtfully for a moment before saying, "We were dating when he got a job at the museum. At first he was really excited. A friend had given him the lead and said it was easy money, and for a while, it seemed like a dream come true. He worked the night shift, but he was always a night owl anyway. Plus, we were in college, and you know what kind of hours college kids keep. So it worked out well for a while. He said he just sat in a room and did his reading for class, and got paid to do it."

"Was that all he did as a night guard?" Hannah asked. "Sit in the guard room and watch screens—or do homework, or whatever?"

"He got up once an hour to walk the floor and make sure nothing was amiss, but otherwise, that was pretty much the job. One night, someone rang the bell on the side door."

"Was that unusual?"

"From what I understand, yes," Janice said. "Albert said it had never happened before, at least during his shift. It probably happened a lot during the day if I had to guess. But he went to investigate, and when he spoke to the people on the intercom, they identified themselves as Frankfort police officers. So he opened the door, because what else can you do when the police are at your door?"

"I read that he wasn't supposed to let anyone in at all," Hannah said. "That that was part of his training."

"Right," Janice said. "But again, these were police officers. Or he thought they were anyway, and you don't say no to police. When two uniformed police officers said they needed to come inside, Albert believed them."

"I read that he didn't ask to see their badges. Is that right?"

Janice sighed. "That was one of the things he spent the rest of his life wishing he could do differently. People fixated on that to show that he must have been in on it, but I always thought that even if he had asked, I'm sure they had fake badges on them. They had the whole getup, with the uniforms and everything, so why wouldn't they have fake badges as well?"

"That's an interesting point. Did anyone find out whether they did bring fake identification?"

"Not that I know of," Janice said. "As soon as they got inside, the police pulled a gun on Albert and tied him up, so he never got a chance to ask. He had nightmares for years. He'd wake up crying, thrashing all over the bed. And who could blame him? Being held at gunpoint and tied up while masked men did who knows what? It was a traumatic experience for him, as I imagine it would have been for anyone."

Hannah had to agree.

"He wasn't the same afterward," Janice said sadly. "Especially when, as I said, people started blaming him for the theft and saying he was in on it."

"He wasn't, then?"

"No." Janice shook her head. "Albert wasn't a thief. It really affected him, everyone thinking he was. Everywhere he went, he felt people staring at him, whispering about him. People even came out and asked him where he kept the paintings and what bank account he'd put the cash in. It was pretty obnoxious, and that kind of thing wears you down after a while."

"You said he changed after the theft. How so?"

"He became withdrawn, for one thing. He wanted to stay in all the time and never go out. Stopped spending time with his friends. He was jumpy—every little noise set him off. Eventually, he dropped out of school and kind of gave up hope. I tried to help as best I could, but I didn't know how. My parents encouraged me to break up with him, but I couldn't leave him like that, not when he was at his lowest."

"So what did you do?"

"I married him instead." She gave a sad, mirthless laugh. "Which, in case you're wondering, is not a good idea. Don't marry a man because you feel bad for him."

"Good advice." Hannah surreptitiously ran her thumb over her engagement ring, glad that no part of her felt bad for Liam.

Janice cracked a genuine smile. "I thought I could save him. My therapist has since helped me see that I never could, and that I need to forgive myself for thinking I could and not being able to. I was young too, and I genuinely wanted to do right by him. But Albert was not in a good place. The marriage only lasted three years, and that was two and a half more than it should have."

"I'm sorry." Whatever Janice's reasons for marrying Albert, it was always sad when two people couldn't make it work. No one ever went into marriage thinking it was going to end in divorce.

"It was for the best that it ended, really. By that point Albert was drinking too much and couldn't hold down a job. We were fighting all the time. The police investigation and media attention had taken over his life, and the lawyer his parents hired to represent him had done his best, but there was no money left. I had to leave, or I was going to drown. But I felt like such a failure, as if I'd messed everything up forever. I was so embarrassed and sad for a long time. But I got through it, and Albert did too. He eventually got sober and started talking to someone about what he'd been through, and I think he ended up okay in the end. And of course I met Bryan, who taught me what a healthy relationship could be like, and here we are."

"Did you keep in touch with Albert?"

"Just here and there. Nothing much. I went to see him in the hospital when he was sick, and that was helpful. We talked about the past and what had gone wrong, and it was healing for both of us."

"I'm so glad."

"Me too." She sighed. "So I've told you what I know. Now tell me about the paintings. How did they end up on Bluegrass Hollow Farm?"

"That's what I'm trying to figure out," Hannah said. "We don't know."

"And you wondered if Albert might have had something to do with it."

Hannah couldn't read her hostess's tone. "Well, the connection was worth looking into."

Janice nodded. "Of course. You'd be crazy not to have asked. Here's what I can tell you. As far as I know, Albert was never inside any cottage on that land. He may have been after the divorce, but I am certain he never had those paintings in his possession. The way he agonized over what happened, and the way it all changed him—you can't fake that. Especially not to your wife."

Hannah wanted to tread lightly here, but she had to ask. "Is there any chance it was not fear and shame, but guilt, that changed him?"

"I really don't think so," Janice said. "He would have to have been an exceptional actor to pull that off, and he was not. He spent the rest of his life wishing he had done something different that night."

Regret didn't rule out guilt, as far as Hannah was concerned. It could be a byproduct of guilt as well. But Janice was certain, and Hannah didn't see how she could discount her opinion. Janice had known Albert better than anyone, and if she—his ex-wife, who obviously didn't have great feelings about him—didn't think he could have been involved, her instinct was probably worth respecting.

"Do you have any idea how the paintings could have ended up there?" Hannah asked.

Janice shook her head. "Not a single one. I assume Albert is the only connection between the cottage and the museum?"

Hannah wasn't about to tell Janice that there was another potential connection in Geraldine Steele.

Luckily, Janice didn't seem to be waiting for an answer. "If you want to know the honest truth, the rumors that it was an inside job never felt too far off to me. It's just that Albert wasn't the insider."

"You mean, you think someone else at the museum was behind the theft? Why?"

"The museum wasn't doing well financially, and those paintings were insured to the teeth," Janice said. "Albert's lawyer dug into it at the time, trying to present a different theory about what happened. He made a pretty convincing case, as I recall. Not that the police ever followed up on it, as far as I can tell. I still have the file here if you want to see it."

"You do?"

Janice nodded. "Just copies, of course. Albert kept the original file, and I have no idea where that went. But I made copies before the divorce. I don't even know why really, except that he was so unstable, and I had a feeling it might be a good idea to have them. Would you like to take a look?"

"I would love that."

"I'll go grab it." Janice pushed herself up and walked out of the room.

The orange-and-white cat rubbed against Hannah's legs, and she reached down and stroked its head gently. It purred loudly, leaning into the caress.

"Here it is." Janice returned with a manila folder. "Do you want to take it with you so you can really go through it?"

"Maybe I should just take pictures of the pages, if the police are coming to talk to you. They may want to see the file too."

"Good thinking."

Hannah set the file on the table and opened it. It was filled with pages of handwritten notes and photocopies of forms. She opened the scanner app on her phone and scanned the pages—there had to be at least two dozen of them—without looking too closely at them. She would dive in later. When she finished scanning, she set the pages back and closed the folder.

"Thank you so much for your help," Hannah said.

"I hope you find out what happened," Janice said. "It would have meant the world to Albert to have his name cleared. I hope you can do it."

"I'll do my best," Hannah promised.

Hopefully these files contained something that could point her in the right direction.

Chapter Seventeen

Hannah wanted to look through the files on her phone the moment she got into her car, but she had to get back to do some work at the restaurant. As she drove, she replayed the conversation in her mind, trying to figure out where it left her.

If Janice was right, Albert had had nothing to do with the theft. He had been an innocent victim who'd made a grave mistake and suffered for it the rest of his life. It was only one person's account, so it didn't necessarily prove anything. But as Hannah thought about it from all angles, she couldn't think of a single reason for Janice to lie. Janice hadn't been implicated in any of the reports she'd seen, Albert was long gone, and the couple had divorced years ago. If anything, it seemed to Hannah that an ex-wife would be *more* likely to suggest her ex's guilt than to insist he was innocent. If Janice was telling the truth—and Hannah believed she was—then the Albert theory was a dead end. His connection to Bluegrass Hollow Farm was mere coincidence.

A pretty incredible coincidence, sure, but nothing more than that.

Going through the lawyer's papers was the next step. If there was evidence that someone inside the museum was involved in the theft, Geraldine Steele would emerge as the primary person of interest. But Hannah was still waiting to hear back from several of the people who had lived in the cottage over the years, and the idea of organized crime being behind the heist now seemed way less far-fetched than it had at first.

Hannah parked and went up to her apartment to change and get ready for work. She headed downstairs and into the restaurant, where the smell of sizzling bacon told her that Jacob was already at work in the kitchen.

She switched on the lights in the dining room and wandered through the quiet restaurant toward the back. She loved being here when it was mostly empty, before the hubbub of the dinner rush started, and she could take a moment to be grateful for this place. Her own restaurant. Her dream, at long last, come true.

Of course, she also liked it when the dining room was full of paying customers. That was a good feeling too, and one that actually paid the bills.

She ducked into the kitchen and found Jacob pounding chicken breasts flat on the stainless-steel table.

"What did that poor chicken ever do to you?" she asked as she walked in.

"Hi, Hannah." The head chef looked up and smiled. "How are you?"

"I'm doing all right. Ready for another week. What's the chicken for?"

"I've been thinking about a new recipe I'd like to try for chicken and waffles," Jacob explained.

"Those are two of my favorite things."

"Is it all right if I try it out a few times tonight and see if people like it?"

"You'd better start with me. Quality control, obviously."

"Naturally." Jacob grinned and plugged in the waffle iron he must have brought from home. "If this takes off, we'll need to get a commercial waffle iron, but I figured I could start with this."

"I'll go get to work on invoices in the office. Will you let me know when it's ready?"

"Of course."

Hannah went into the office, sat down at her computer, and was going through her emails—bill, spam, price hike on chicken—when her phone rang. It was a number she didn't recognize, with a Lexington area code. Normally she wouldn't pick it up, but Joanie Gardner, now White, lived in Lexington, according to her mother. She would risk it.

"Hello?"

"Hi, is this Hannah Prentiss?"

"Yes?"

"This is Joanie White. My mother told me you were trying to get in touch with me and said you're a friend of Christine Knicely."

"That's right," Hannah said. "Christine's daughter, Lacy, is actually my best friend, and Christine is like a second mom to me."

"In that case, I'm delighted to meet you. How is Christine?" Joanie's voice was warm, and she came across as friendly and outgoing.

"She's doing well," Hannah said. "Lacy's six months pregnant, and Christine is very excited to become a grandmother."

"Of course she is. She always loved her family so much. That's wonderful news." Joanie laughed. "It's hard to believe Lacy is old enough to have a child of her own."

"Yep. She's in her midthirties now and runs the farm with her husband of over a decade. He also has a bookshop in town."

"Oh dear. Does that mean…?" She didn't finish the thought, but Hannah guessed what she meant.

"Yes, Frank passed away some years ago," Hannah said.

"I'm very sorry to hear that. Frank was a good man."

"He was the best," Hannah agreed.

"I'm glad Lacy wanted to take over the farm, though. It would have been a shame for that farm to leave their family."

"Lacy loves it there. She's mostly raising chickens to sell their eggs, and she's doing a great business."

"I'm so glad to hear it. Does Christine still live on the farm as well?"

"Not at the moment. She moved into town after Frank died and Lacy and Neil took over the main house. But she's moving into the cottage on the property so she can be nearby when the baby is born."

"That's wonderful. I remember that cottage well from when I stayed there. It's so cute, and it's wonderful that she'll be nearby to help with the baby. I'm thrilled for her."

"I'm excited for her too. For them all."

Before Hannah could figure out a way to steer the conversation where she needed it to go, Joanie said, "Can I ask you a question?"

"Of course."

"I've loved hearing about Christine and Lacy. But why are you the one calling me, rather than Christine?"

Hannah laughed. "That's a totally fair question. And the answer is a bit complicated. Lacy and Neil are in the process of renovating the cottage for Christine, and they found something strange behind some of the drywall."

Joanie gasped. "What did they find?"

"Some paintings, actually."

"Oh. Thank goodness." Joanie let out a breath. "I was afraid you were going to say something horrifying. Paintings are so much better than what I expected. But wait. Why would anyone put paintings behind drywall?"

"It turns out they were stolen from an art museum."

"For real?"

"It's true," Hannah said. "A museum in Frankfort, Kentucky."

"An art heist? I didn't know that was a thing that happened in real life. I thought it was just something in movies."

"This was very real," Hannah said. "And somehow, two of the paintings that were stolen ended up in the cottage on the farm—"

"*Two* paintings?"

"Two important and very valuable paintings. We're trying to understand how they got there. I'm talking to everyone who stayed in the cottage to see if anyone knows what happened."

"Oh, are you with the police? Do you need me to make an official statement of some kind?"

"No, I'm not with the police," Hannah said. "I'm helping in a more informal capacity."

"Good. I'd rather talk to Christine's friend than the police. How can I help?"

"Well, I guess we wanted to know whether you ever saw or heard anything odd while you lived in the cottage."

"Not that I can think of. Wait. Are you saying the paintings were there while I was staying there? There were stolen paintings behind the wall of that cottage the whole time?"

"We don't know exactly when the paintings were hidden in the cottage," Hannah hurried to assure her. "That's one of the things we're trying to work out."

"Well, I certainly didn't know anything about them. How did they even get behind the wall? Did somebody open the walls up and put them back there? Wouldn't you want to look at them or sell them or something? I don't understand the point of stealing paintings from an art museum just to hide them away."

"I don't understand it myself," Hannah admitted. "That's the other part of what we're trying to understand."

"Well, I wish I could help, but I'm afraid all I have is questions," Joanie said. "If the pictures were there when I lived there, I didn't know about it. I sure wish I had. The walls were pretty bare while I was there."

Hannah wanted to laugh at the image of a younger Joanie hanging priceless Edward Hicks and Thomas Cole paintings on the walls, without any idea of their value or provenance.

"If you do think of anything odd that happened while you lived there, or anything that seems like it could be related, will you please let me know?"

"Of course. And Hannah?"

"Yes?"

"I'd love to be in contact with Christine again. Do you happen to have her information?"

"How about I ask her to call you?"

"That'll work. Thank you," Joanie said.

After Hannah ended the call, she mulled over the conversation and didn't see any red flags or anything that seemed odd. Joanie appeared to be totally surprised by the news.

It wasn't proof that Joanie was innocent by any means. But Hannah was pretty good at reading people, and she didn't think there was much chance Joanie was behind the hidden paintings. She crossed Joanie off her mental list, then turned back to the computer.

She had only managed to pay one invoice before Jacob appeared with a plate of crispy fried chicken sitting on a fluffy waffle dripping with syrup.

"That looks amazing."

"Wait until you taste it."

Hannah set the plate on her desk and cut off a bite with the knife and fork he handed her. "Oh wow." It was sweet and crispy and salty and so, so good.

"You like it?"

"I don't know. I'd better take another bite to make sure." She took another bite, and it was somehow even better.

"It's good, right? I think our customers would like this dish."

"I think they'll love it." After a third bite, she set her knife and fork down while she chewed.

"So it's okay to try it out on a few customers today?"

Hannah pretended to consider the question. "I think so."

Jacob laughed and returned to the kitchen. Hannah went back to her invoices and managed to polish off the food in the process. She took her plate to the kitchen, glad to see Dylan was already in the dining room rolling silverware and Raquel was refilling the salt and pepper shakers.

She was headed to her office again when she saw Neil walking past the big plate glass windows. Hannah hurried outside to catch him. "Neil!"

Neil turned and smiled. "Hi, Hannah."

"Hi. What's the story with the cottage?"

His smile faltered. "I assume Lacy told you someone broke in again last night."

"She did. They took more tools?"

"Yep. Gus is mad. Not as us, thankfully, but at the situation."

"I would be as well. That's two sets of tools that have been stolen. They aren't cheap."

"Yeah. I guess the lesson here is to not leave tools in the cottage overnight, but that doesn't explain how anyone knew they were there. It's not as if the cottage is on some major thoroughfare where lots of people could have seen that Gus had brought new tools by. So how did the thief know the tools were there, and why did he take them, but once again leave the copper wire?"

"Either your thief doesn't understand the value of copper wire, or his interest is not in the value of what he's stealing."

"In which case, it's probably about stopping work on the cottage," Neil said. "I have to admit, I'm starting to think there might be some merit to that idea."

"But why?" Hannah asked. "We've already found two paintings. Is there something else in the cottage that someone doesn't want you to find?"

"That's an intriguing idea." Neil said. "I don't know what else there could be, but that would make sense."

"So the question is, what is it?"

"Right." Neil nodded. "And, obviously, who? And that's what I'm working on now."

"Oh yeah?"

"Well, hopefully. I'm headed to the hardware store now to get a trail camera. Mike Solis told me they have them in stock. We're going to set that up and see if it catches anyone outside the cottage."

"That's a good idea," Hannah said. "One of the ones with night vision?"

"That's what I'm hoping for, since the thefts seem to happen overnight."

"I hope this leads to some answers."

"Me too." Neil let out a long breath. "By the time the police left today, it wasn't even worth starting on the demolition. Plus Gus needs to go out and get more tools *again*, so we're now looking at starting tomorrow. Lacy is getting anxious because she really wants her mom to be moved in before the baby comes. We should still have a few months, but renovations and babies don't tend to operate on strict schedules."

"I understand," Hannah said. "Let's hope it doesn't happen again. Or if it does, that your trail cam catches someone in the act."

"Let's hope." Neil started off again.

"Tell Lacy I said hi," Hannah called. Neil promised he would, and she headed back inside.

When she returned to the dining room, Hannah looked around and saw that Raquel had finished with the salt and pepper shakers and was placing them on the tables. But she was moving slowly, rather than at her usual brisk pace, and she seemed distracted. Hannah walked over to her.

"Is everything all right, Raquel?"

"Hmm?" Raquel looked up at her. "Oh, sorry. I guess I was in another world. I'll get my head in the game, I promise."

"Are you okay?"

"I'm fine." She sighed. "I was just thinking about Marshall, is all."

"How is he doing?"

"He likes the job. This long-distance thing is harder than I thought, but we're making it work." She gave a weak smile.

Hannah didn't believe her, but it was too close to opening time to press the waitress.

Once the doors opened and customers started being seated, Raquel regained her focus. Tuesday nights weren't usually too busy, but between a big group that came in after a church basketball game and a group of women celebrating a birthday, the dining room filled up quickly. Raquel received a round of cheers when she brought out a special plate of chicken and waffles for the birthday girl to try on the house. By the time they were halfway through the dinner hour, Dylan hadn't dropped anything or mixed up any orders as he tended to do, and Hannah was starting to think this might be a pretty good night.

But then, shortly after seven, Elaine called Hannah over to the hostess stand, and Hannah saw that Colin Steele stood with her. He didn't look happy. She felt her stomach drop. Whatever was happening, he wasn't here with good news.

"Hello, Colin," she said, trying to put on her usual welcoming smile. "A table for one?"

"I'm not here for dinner, Hannah." He looked around the room. "Is there some place we can talk privately?"

"Is something wrong?"

The sheriff didn't answer.

Hannah nodded and led him to her office at the back of the restaurant, pulling the door most of the way closed behind him.

Colin stepped forward and leveled his eyes at her. "This art heist isn't a joke, Hannah. You don't understand what you're dealing with here. This is not some lost piece of antique jewelry or some anonymous letters. This is not the kind of thing someone other than the police should be getting involved with."

She knew he wasn't trying to belittle the cases she'd solved in the past, but his words still stung.

His expression softened, and he added, "Hannah, I don't want you to get hurt."

She stared at him, open-mouthed. Nothing she'd found had indicated that there was any kind of current danger surrounding this case. What did he know that he wasn't telling her?

Colin sighed. "Just believe me, please. And please don't interfere with our investigation. Now, I know you're busy, so I'll see myself out."

She didn't follow him. Instead, she stood in the office for a moment, trying to collect her thoughts. Sheriff Steele had told her to back off and warned her that she could get hurt. The whole exchange was out of character for him. He'd never spoken so brusquely to her before. The investigation seemed to be hitting a sore spot.

Hannah pulled out her phone and called Liam.

"Colin Steele just came by the restaurant," she said when he picked up. "He told me in so many words that he was worried I could get hurt if I keep investigating."

"Whoa. Really?" There was noise in the background. It sounded like the guys were cheering for some kind of game on the TV, but it got quieter by the second. He must be walking to somewhere more private.

"Yeah. He seemed pretty upset. He came all the way in here to tell me to stop."

"What are you going to do?" Liam said.

He was asking whether she intended to listen to the sheriff. Did she care about Colin's warning?

"I don't actually know," Hannah finally admitted. Was she going to stop trying to find answers because of his warning? Was she willing to just forget it all and let the police investigate?

Hannah realized the truth before the thought was even fully formed. No, she did not intend to stop asking questions. She would stay out of Colin's way and not get involved in his investigation, and she would not do anything to put his work or the case at risk.

But if she could learn a few things without getting in the way of what the police were working on, she owed it to Lacy and Christine to keep going.

She could hardly stop now.

Chapter Eighteen

H annah was taking the trash out to the dumpster that night when her phone rang. She answered at once when she saw her friend's name on the screen. "Hi, Margot."

"Hey," Margot replied. "I know it's late there but I had a minute, so thought I would call and see if there was any update on that art. I'm dying to know if you found out how it got into that cottage."

"Not yet," Hannah said. "Though the police are working on it." No sense in broadcasting that she was trying to figure it out as well.

"I was reading about it, and it's so crazy, isn't it? Have you listened to the podcast yet?"

"Yes, I'm four episodes in," Hannah said.

"I binged it. It sounds like maybe the mob was involved, and that the guard was in on it?"

"I actually don't think the guard was involved," Hannah said. "I mean, obviously I'm not the police, so that's not an official finding or anything. But I talked to the guard's ex-wife. They were together at the time, and she thinks he didn't have anything to do with it. That what he went through that night changed him."

"And you believe her?"

"I do. I don't think she had any reason to lie."

"Well, maybe it was the mob after all. Did you get to the episode where they found that the Mafia guy had a list of all the paintings?"

"No, but I knew about that. I still can't get over the idea that Kentucky used to have a mob problem. And I can see how the mob could have been involved in the theft. The problem is that I don't see how they would have had any connection to Lacy's cottage," Hannah said. "That's what makes this particular theory so hard for me to believe."

"So what do you think happened?" Margot asked.

"I don't know," Hannah confessed.

"Okay, well, my real question was this: I heard on the podcast that one of the paintings—the Rothko—was found in a New York apartment like ten years ago. Which is crazy, because who displays stolen art and then invites people over to see it? How dumb can you be?"

"People keep saying that, but I don't know. What else would you do with it? What's the point of having a Rothko if no one ever sees it?"

Margot laughed. "There are lots of reasons. For one, most expensive art is bought as an investment these days rather than a display piece. But some people genuinely love the art or the artist. In the case of stolen artwork, someone might have it and even display it in their home, to show it off to a small circle of friends or other oligarchs or whatever, but it would never be seen publicly. It's the whole thing about inviting *lots* of people over—some of whom were not vetted—that's odd. Most stolen art would never be displayed casually like that."

There was a lot to unpack in what Margot suggested, but Hannah tried to focus on the main question she had. "What was that about oligarchs?"

"I just meant that as an example. I don't know if oligarchs were involved here. But most stolen artwork is never seen again, and that's because a lot of it leaves the country and is very hard to track afterward. There are plenty of people with a lot of money who want the status symbol of having a Vermeer or a Degas or a Picasso in their collection. They'll pay for the privilege, but they're usually smart enough to keep quiet about it once the piece is in their possession. It's never spotted, so it's never found. What's unusual is that this one was."

Hannah probably shouldn't be surprised that most stolen art was never seen again, but it was a depressing thought. The work of these American masters just gone.

Except, in this case, a few of the paintings had been recovered.

"So how did it end up on that wall in New York?" Hannah asked.

"Right," Margot said. "And why did this guy end up exposing it instead of keeping it out of view like most people would have?"

"It's unclear, based on what I heard, whether he knew the work was stolen," Hannah said. "Maybe he genuinely wasn't aware."

"He absolutely knew," Margot said. "He had to. It came from a fake gallery."

"It did?"

"Yeah, they didn't go into this on the podcast, but he bought the painting from a gallery called Kingfisher. I've never heard of it, and it would be very unusual for a gallery I've never heard of to have sold a Rothko. I mean, probably if it had been Saatchi or Gagosian or Hauser and Wirth, it wouldn't have stood out, but—"

"Those are galleries?"

"Quite famous ones. The ones that typically handle sales of work at this level. Or an auction house like Sotheby's or Christie's might. But not one that I've never heard of. So I started looking into Kingfisher, and I couldn't find it. It doesn't show up in any of our databases or registries. It never showed at any of the art fairs, and there is no record of any significant sales in the trades."

"So what does that mean?"

"I'm sure the police have already discovered this, so I don't think I'm breaking any news here, but it's obviously a front. A fake gallery set up to sell the stolen painting, or perhaps more than one stolen painting."

"Why wouldn't the podcast or the newspaper articles I've read mention that?"

"No idea. Maybe they didn't know, or maybe there was a legal reason not to. The police keep things back from the public during an investigation, right? Or sometimes journalists don't print details that can't be verified to avoid the risk of a libel lawsuit. I would guess it's like that. All I know is that Kingfisher isn't a gallery anyone in the art world has ever heard of, so if it were me, I would be looking into who is behind that."

Hannah thought for a moment, then said, "You just mentioned all these art world tools that mean nothing to me. If I had the name of someone who worked at a gallery in New York, would you be able to find that person for me?"

"Is it someone connected to the stolen art?"

"Possibly. I don't really know."

"What's the name? I'll see what I can find."

"Dickie McAllister." That was Monty Carlyle's friend in the art world. The one who had a meteoric career rise right around the time the paintings were stolen.

"I'll look into it."

"Thanks, Margo."

Hannah hung up and went back inside the restaurant. Though she laughed and joked with Elaine and Raquel as they finished getting the dining room ready for the next day, her mind was occupied with thoughts about how most stolen paintings were never seen again. How had those paintings ended up, not listed on the black market for millions, but hidden in a cottage in Blackberry Valley? It made no sense.

After she locked up and went upstairs, Hannah was restless and anxious. She was exhausted, but she also knew she wouldn't be able to go to sleep because her mind spun with the case. She could read a book or watch an episode of a show she liked. Instead, she decided to pull up the files Janice had given her that morning. Albert's ex-wife said they contained copies of his lawyer's files. She doubted it, but if the files were dry and dull, maybe reading them would help her sleep.

The first photos showed invoices from a Charles M. Flora, Esq. The total probably wasn't exorbitant for a lawyer's fee, but it was a higher number than she suspected a college student moonlighting as a museum guard would have been able to pay comfortably, and Hannah wondered if Albert had gotten help from a relative or friends to cover the cost. But she didn't see how that would be relevant, so she thumbed to the photos of the next stack.

Below that was a file containing a stapled packet of what looked like photocopies of notes handwritten on a legal pad. The first page listed the paintings that had been taken in the theft—a list that was now familiar to Hannah—and their approximate values. It was, as she had known, quite a large sum. She assumed these were their values at the time of the theft and that they would be worth even more today, especially given their history.

The next document showed a hand-drawn diagram of the museum, with the rooms sketched out in pencil and the approximate location of each of the paintings marked. That was interesting to see, actually.

According to this map, there were four galleries on each of two floors. Seven of the paintings that had been stolen were displayed on the second floor, while three were on the first, and they were scattered throughout the galleries. As the security camera footage showed, the thieves had known which ones they wanted and where to find them.

Hannah studied the map for a few minutes, which was helpful for visualizing the space, but she couldn't see any clues that she hadn't known before, so she kept reading.

The next pages exhibited what appeared to be a list of names handwritten on a lined legal pad. Some of the names were familiar to Hannah—Vinnie Amelio, the mobster suspected to have been involved, Montgomery Carlyle, Geraldine's dad and board chair—while most were totally meaningless to her.

She scanned the list, looking for any that jumped out. Mason Fiorello, Anthony Padua, Gregory Stephanopoulos, Beckett Harmsworth, Jeffrey Bloom, Eleanor Bergen, Yarros Jimenez. Who were these people, and what did they have to do with the theft at the museum?

Or rather, what did the lawyer, Charles Flora, think their involvement was?

A scribbled note in the margins answered her question. It was so faint in the photo that she almost missed it, but she zoomed in and read, *Others interviewed by police in connection with theft.*

There were a handful of legal documents—official court filings, a summons, records of Albert's arrest and release from police custody. Albert had never been officially charged with the crime, so the case had never gone to court, but there were plenty of records that left a legal paper trail as the case against him advanced.

After the legal paperwork was what appeared to be a transcript of a tape recording conducted by Mr. Flora. The first few pages were simply Albert giving his account of what had happened the night of the theft. Hannah read it carefully, but it matched what she had already learned: Albert believed the men were police officers, he didn't recognize them, he was tied up at gunpoint and left until the morning. But she kept reading, hoping there might be something new.

She stopped when she came to a section where the lawyer asked Albert about his experience working at the museum.

> FLORA: *How long had you been working at the museum at the time of the theft?*
>
> JOHNSTON: *Two months, give or take.*
>
> FLORA: *Were you always on the night shift?*
>
> JOHNSTON: *Mostly. I'm a night owl, so the hours were good, and I could get other things done in between sweeps. It was good in that way.*
>
> FLORA: *You said mostly. What did you do for the museum besides working night shift?*
>
> JOHNSTON: *Special events. Sometimes they would have these fundraisers and special after-hours events for the muckety-mucks, and they hired extra security for those. At first I didn't understand why they needed more security for the rich donors than they did when the regular people came in, but then Idris explained that the rich people liked to see a lot of guards. Made them feel good about how secure the place was so they could feel safe giving money.*

FLORA: Who's Idris?

JOHNSTON: Another guard. He's been there for a few years.

FLORA: So Idris was saying that having more guards around wasn't really making the place any safer?

JOHNSTON: I mean, sure, it would have been hard for someone to get away with stealing anything with so many guards around. But we weren't exactly worried about the rich donors stealing the artwork. [laughs] Not at a fundraiser anyway.

FLORA: What do you mean by that?

JOHNSTON: I mean, those guys would be more subtle than that, wouldn't they? They wouldn't take the art off the wall at a gathering with other people around. If they were going to steal the artwork, they'd do it another way, wouldn't they?

FLORA: What would they do?

JOHNSTON: Look, I may not have seen anyone stealing artwork at a party, but it doesn't mean I didn't hear things.

FLORA: You might as well be frank with me, Albert. I'm on your side. What did you hear?

JOHNSTON: The museum was in financial trouble. I heard the museum director, Eleanor, and that Carlyle guy talking about a hole in the budget that they needed to fill. He was talking about how they had all these valuable works of art on the walls, but were struggling to keep the lights on and said the expenses were going up. She was worried that she would lose her job if she didn't come through with the money to pay expenses, and Carlyle said he had it under control.

FLORA: What do you think he meant by that?

JOHNSTON: *At the time, I didn't have any idea. I was just trying to stay out of the way, you know? But after it all went down, I thought about it, and I remembered something else Idris told me. He said how it wouldn't have mattered if one of the paintings did go missing because they were so heavily insured that the museum would come out ahead.*

FLORA: *Is that true?*

JOHNSTON: *I have no idea. I just know he said that, and I thought about that conversation between Eleanor and Carlyle a lot after the theft.*

So Albert had believed the heist had been an inside job too—just not in the way that meant the security guard was involved. But Hannah didn't see anything in the following notes that resembled anything like proof of the theory. It was a good one, totally plausible, but Albert obviously hadn't had any way to prove it, or he would have been able to clear his name.

Hannah kept reading, and their conversation eventually turned to the organized crime theory.

FLORA: *Do you know the name Vinnie Amelio?*

JOHNSTON: *I hadn't heard of him until the police started trying to get me to confess that I was working for him. I'm not, by the way. I'd never heard of the guy. I don't know anything about the mob beyond what you get in fiction. I don't know why they think the mob might be involved.*

FLORA: *There's a lot of money at stake.*

JOHNSTON: *Yeah, but art? Doesn't the mob deal with things like drugs or gambling or, I don't know, sanitation? Since when is the mob interested in Georgia O'Keefe? She painted flowers, for heaven's sake.*

FLORA: *Since a Georgia O'Keefe painting recently sold at auction for over $16 million, it's worth investigating.*

JOHNSTON: *It did?*

FLORA: *Think the mob might be interested in flowers now?*

JOHNSTON: *I guess they might be for that price.*

Hannah read through the rest of the interview, and though it touched on several theories that had already come up, she didn't end up with any new leads.

She set down her phone and sat back, stretching her arms above her head. She was tired enough now that she thought she might actually be able to go to sleep. It was interesting to see the notes from Albert's lawyer, but she wasn't sure it got her any closer to finding the truth.

Pushing herself up, she got ready for bed, and when she checked her phone again, she saw that she'd missed a phone call from Liam. It was probably too late to call him back at this point. Instead, she sent him a text and climbed into bed.

She tried to empty her mind, but she couldn't make herself stop thinking about everything she'd read, trying to connect the dots. It felt like there was something right there, just beyond her grasp, but no matter how hard she tried, she couldn't quite wrap her fingers around it.

What was she missing?

Chapter Nineteen

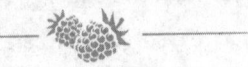

The discovery of the artwork at Lacy's farm was on the front page of *Blackberry Valley Chronicle* Wednesday morning. Jack Delaney, the editor-in-chief, had interviewed Lacy and Neil, as well as Jacky and Colin about the discovery. There was a photo of the hole in the wall where the paintings had been found, along with a picture of Lacy and Neil in front of the cottage and a picture of the Witherspoon Museum.

Hannah called Lacy when she had finished reading the article. "When did Jack come by and interview you?"

"Monday," Lacy said. "I can't believe I forgot to mention it to you."

"We've all been a little distracted. I'm interested to see if the article turns up anything as far as clues."

"What kind of clue would come out because of that article?"

"I don't know. Maybe someone has known all along how the paintings got there, but didn't realize someone else was wondering. But now that they see the newspaper, they'll come forward with what they know."

"And maybe I'll win the lottery," Lacy teased.

"Hey, you never know what could happen, and I'm glad it's in the paper. It can only help."

"We'll see." There was a noise like a gate slamming on Lacy's end of the phone, and a moment later she was surrounded by the soft clucking sound that told Hannah she was in the chicken coop. "Anyway, good news. We're going to start demolition again today, hopefully for real this time."

"I'm glad to hear it. Let's hope Gus can make up for lost time."

"I just pray that nothing more gets stolen from the cottage. And Neil put up the trail camera, so if anything does happen, at least we might be able to catch it on video this time."

"Ideally it won't come to that," Hannah said.

"Amen." The clucking noises got louder. "Sorry, I've got to go. Eggatha is following me around like a, well, like a chicken with her head cut off, trying to get to the food in my bucket."

"Let's hope Eggatha keeps her head. Have a good day." Hannah hung up, enjoying the image of one of Lacy's favorite chickens chasing her pregnant friend around the pen.

Opening her laptop, Hannah ran a search for the stolen tools once again. She checked all the places she'd checked before, but didn't come up with a match.

She finally pushed herself up. She had to get ready for her meeting with Nicole.

Nicole and Owen lived in a Queen Anne home surrounded by lush landscaping, a few blocks from the university campus. Hannah wasn't sure what to expect, but when Nicole welcomed her into the house, she found it decorated with tasteful modern furniture and beautiful antique rugs. The only evidence of Nicole's passion for insects was a framed photo of a butterfly wing over the fireplace.

"Thank you so much for meeting with me," Hannah said as Nicole ushered her toward a soft gray tuxedo couch.

"It's no problem. I'm sorry Owen couldn't be here as well, but he's teaching a class this morning," Nicole said. She was probably in her late fifties or early sixties, with short silver hair and a kind face. "I have to admit, I'm intrigued. I talked to someone from the sheriff's office yesterday, and it was clear they'd found something in that old cottage and wanted to know if we'd put it there, but he couldn't say what it was."

"You already talked to the sheriff? Oh good."

"Yes. They came by yesterday, and I spoke to a very nice man. But I was so confused by the end of it. We couldn't imagine what they'd found in that cottage. I thought it must be something illegal, and Owen thought it was probably a large amount of cash. But then we saw that article in the paper this morning and saw that it was a couple of paintings."

"That's right." If Nicole had seen the story, no one could accuse Hannah of being the one who spilled the beans.

"That's odd, isn't it?"

"It is indeed," Hannah said.

"And how are you related to all this?"

Hannah explained her connection to Lacy and Christine, then gave some details about the paintings.

"It's all very exciting," Nicole said when Hannah was done. "And I wish I could tell you something useful, especially after you've come all this way, but I'm afraid I really don't know a thing about it. If those paintings were in the cottage while we lived there, we didn't know it."

"There was never any point when the drywall had to come down, or anything like that while you lived there?" Hannah asked.

"I'm afraid not," Nicole said. "And Owen and I are scientists. We don't know a thing about art. We wouldn't have known that those were important paintings even if we'd seen them. We would have thought it was an odd place to store them, behind a wall, but we wouldn't have guessed they were worth millions."

"Can you think of anyone who had access to your house while you lived there?"

"Not really," Nicole said. "No one stayed there while we were out of town or anything like that. We were just working, writing, trying to get tenure." Nicole sighed. "We loved that little cottage in the woods. It was small, but such a pretty setting. And it was perfect for us, being so far away from everything. I'm an entomologist, and I found so many interesting specimens out in those woods. Owen is a botanist, and he was able to plant a little garden and experiment with different fertilizers and things. His work there inspired a book that got him tenure. So it was wonderful. We were newlyweds, and I look back on that time as one of the happiest periods in our lives. But I'm afraid I don't know anything about those paintings."

Hannah believed her. Which was good in that she could cross the Daniels off the list of suspects.

But it was also bad in that the list of suspects was slowly converging around one person she really hoped didn't have any part to play in this crime.

Chapter Twenty

Liam called while Hannah was on her way back to town. *Liam "My Fiancé!" Berthold* flashed on her dashboard screen. She smiled.

"How's it going?" he asked when she answered.

"Okay." She explained who Nicole was and why she'd spoken to her. Then she asked, "What are you up to? You're working today, right?"

"Yep. I'm here at the station. My parents are going to have lunch with Ron and Camille Villaruz today, then Mom is meeting up with some women from her old Bible study this afternoon."

"Your parents have more active social lives than I do."

"They're only here for a week, so they're trying to see as many people as possible. But they don't have plans tomorrow. They saw the article in the paper this morning, and suddenly Mom was reminded how much they love the Witherspoon Museum."

"She's been there?"

"Apparently so, when Mom's mom came to visit before I was born. Anyway, they want to go see it again. I don't work tomorrow, so they wanted to know if we'd like to go with them."

"Of course." And Hannah meant it. She actually couldn't believe she hadn't thought to go see the museum herself before now. Frankfort was only a two-hour drive from Blackberry Valley. She had to work tomorrow, but if they went early, she could go into the restaurant a bit late. "Can we go in the morning?"

"Of course."

"And can Lacy come too?"

"Sure, if you want her to."

"I don't know if she can make it with all that she has going on, but if she can, it would be good for her to see the place to get a better understanding of what happened. Plus, your parents will love her."

"We can pick her up on the way. Just let me know."

"Okay, thanks. I'll ask her now."

"Mom will be thrilled."

"What about your dad?"

"Art museums aren't really his thing, but he'll be okay."

"I hope he likes it."

"It will be great. Let's plan on it."

Hannah listened to two more episodes of *A Brush with Danger* while she got ready for work. The podcast host was really entertaining, perfectly stringing along the listener as she told the story of the theft and interviewed the people who were involved.

In the fifth episode, the host went into the mobster theory in depth, giving some background on Vincent Amelio and discussing his arrests prior to the one that had gotten him locked up for good—theft, larceny, suspected homicide—and how few of the charges had stuck. She also talked about his network of associates without naming any names, and she managed to convey the idea that Vinnie was still very much involved with his network's activities, even in prison.

For a brief moment, Hannah wondered if she should go talk to him. He was incarcerated in Louisville. That wasn't too far away.

But she didn't get very far down that road before she realized it would be a terrible idea. She would definitely be interfering in the sheriff's investigation by meeting with Vinnie. And she could only imagine what Liam would say. Okay, so she wasn't going to run off and go visit a mobster in prison.

But maybe she could still find something. She checked the online auction site she'd looked at before, as well as the local classifieds page, looking for the tools that had been stolen. She didn't find anything there, so she tried the social media site's marketplace.

And there—

Oh, dear.

Hannah called Lacy first, hoping her friend might be able to tell her whether the tools that had been stolen matched the ones listed for sale in the ad she'd found.

"I don't really know," Lacy said. "We'd probably have to ask Gus to be sure. But I'm looking at the post online now, and I can see why you think it looks suspicious."

"The seller is listed as someone in Blackberry Valley," Hannah said. "But it's a brand-new profile, created earlier this week, and this is the first post of any sort from this person. I've never heard of a Jonny Smithers in Blackberry Valley, have you?"

"No. That's got to be a fake name. It sounds too much like John Smith. Plus, what they're selling is two toolboxes with contents included, two table saws—one of which is new in its box—and two sledgehammers. Which I think is basically all that was stolen from the cottage."

"They must be Gus's tools," Hannah said. "Will you give me his number so I can call him and check?"

"You bet." Lacy said. She gave Hannah Gus's number, then they ended their call so Hannah could reach out to the contractor.

Gus picked up right away. "Gus Brody, how can I help you?"

"Hey, Gus, this is Lacy Minyard's friend, Hannah Prentiss. I wanted you to see something." Hannah sent him the link she'd found. "Are those your missing tools?"

"Yes," Gus said, his tone dripping with shock. "The arrogance. Can you even believe that? Listing them for sale publicly, right here in town?"

"It does seem bold," Hannah said.

"How did you find them?" Gus asked. "That was some good sleuthing."

"Just poking around," Hannah said. "If you're sure those are your tools, I'll call the police now and report it."

"If you don't call them, I will."

Hannah called Jacky Holt and sent her the link to the tools, and Jacky promised to look into it. Hannah hung up, feeling a sense of accomplishment for the first time in days. She might not be any closer to figuring out how the paintings ended up in the cottage, but she had done something useful.

Dinner started slowly at the Hot Spot, with only a few tables filled for the first seating, but things picked up after six o'clock. Soon the dining room was so busy that at first Hannah didn't even notice Christine Johnston sitting at a table with a woman Hannah didn't know. Hannah smiled at them, and Christine waved her over.

"Hannah, this is Joanie," Christine said, her eyes sparkling.

"How wonderful," Hannah said, meaning it. "It's great to meet you in person, Joanie."

"You too. I called Christine the minute you sent me her number, and we talked for two hours," Joanie said. "It was so much fun to catch up that we decided we had to continue our chat in person. So I drove up, and here we are."

"You drove all the way out here?" Hannah asked. "That's so great."

"Lexington isn't that far," Joanie said. "Not for an old friend. Besides, I've always loved this part of the state. My grandparents had a cabin out this way when I was a kid, and I adored coming out here. It was like heaven on earth, and some of the happiest days of my life were spent there."

"I remember that cabin!" Christine exclaimed. "It was out on Spring Lake, right?"

"That's it. Remember how we used to run straight off the dock and try to walk on the water?"

"It never seemed to work, but we always thought it might. Your grandmother made the best strawberry shortcake."

"She did, didn't she?" Joanie beamed.

"We've been chatting and laughing up a storm," Christine said. "Just like old times. It reminded me of you and Lacy, truth be told."

Hannah hadn't seen Christine so animated in a long time, and it warmed her heart. Maybe something good had come out of this mess in the end.

"We were chatting about the reason you called me," Joanie said. "Those paintings."

"Joanie was saying she wished she'd known they were there," Christine added.

"You just said they were worth millions! I had just gotten out of a bad marriage, and I'd lost everything. I was so poor I couldn't even afford rent. I would have ended up on the street if you hadn't let me stay in that cottage. If I'd known that every time I was in that kitchen I was inches away from paintings worth millions of dollars, you wouldn't be seeing me around here anymore."

"Because you'd be in prison for selling stolen goods," Christine pointed out.

"No, because I'd be on a Caribbean island somewhere, sipping a drink with a tiny umbrella."

Hannah saw Dylan struggling to balance a tray of plates and figured she'd better get back to work. "You two enjoy your meal," she said, hurrying to give her waiter a hand.

The reunited friends were still at that table, laughing and lingering over desserts, two hours later. It was good to see Christine so happy. Hannah was glad they had reconnected. She might never get to the bottom of what had happened with the paintings, but at least some good would come out of it.

Chapter Twenty-One

———— 🍓 ————

Liam was waiting downstairs with coffee and doughnuts bright and early the next morning.

"This is becoming a habit," Lori joked as Hannah climbed into the back seat next to her. Daniel was there too, against the other door.

"No one is riding up front?" Hannah buckled herself in and closed the door.

"That's for Lacy," Lori said. "Pregnant women get shotgun. And anything else they want, actually."

"Ah. That makes sense." It was sweet, come to think of it.

"You said she's six months along?" Lori asked.

"That's right. Due in August."

"How exciting. A baby is the best thing in the world. But an August baby—she has to make it through the whole hot summer. That's rough."

"Do you want kids?" Daniel asked from the far side of the rear seat.

"Yes," Hannah said. "I do. Not right away, but definitely."

"Sometimes kids don't come when you expect them to," Daniel said.

Hannah had no idea how to respond to that. How had she managed to say something wrong already?

"We trust that God will bring us a baby in His time," Liam said smoothly from the front seat. "It may be sooner or later than we would hope, but God's timing is always the best."

"Exactly," Hannah agreed gratefully.

"You two will have the most gorgeous children," Lori said. "I can't wait to be a grandmother. But I'll have to wait for a while at least, won't I? Oh, it would be so hard to be far away with a grand-baby around. Daniel, we might need to sell the place in Florida and move back when the baby comes."

"Let's not put the house on the market just yet," Daniel said.

Lori started telling stories about Liam as an infant. He had apparently been the sweetest and most beautiful baby in the world, so perhaps that would pass to any children he and Hannah had. When they got to Bluegrass Hollow Farm and Lacy climbed into the front seat, Lori peppered her with questions about how she was feeling, how the pregnancy had been so far, and whether Lacy and Neil had picked out baby names, so the drive passed quickly. In no time, Liam was pulling off the highway and driving through the streets of Frankfort.

Frankfort was a beautiful town, with charming red-brick buildings making up most of the downtown and the dome of the capital building soaring over it all. People often assumed Lexington or Louisville were the capital of Kentucky, but Frankfort held that distinction. The seat of government was a picturesque and well-maintained town filled with great restaurants, historic sites, and museums.

The Witherspoon Museum was housed in a three-story brick building on a corner just off one of the main streets in the historic downtown. Liam parked, and they walked to the front to buy tickets. Before going in, Hannah ducked around the side of the building, where a metal door was set into the wall. A small buzzer panel and a keypad were set to the side.

"So this is where the thieves went in, huh?" Lacy murmured, coming up beside her.

"It must be," Hannah said, recalling what she'd seen in the grainy security camera footage. She looked up and found the camera positioned over the door.

Hannah and Lacy headed back toward the front of the museum, where Liam and his parents were waiting. "Ready?" Liam asked.

Hannah nodded.

The inside of the museum had soaring ceilings and bright white walls. Hannah picked up a brochure that contained a map of the space, and she saw that it matched the sketch she'd seen in the notes from Albert's lawyer's files.

"It looks like the collection flows roughly in chronological order, with the earliest works on the ground floor and later works on the second floor," Hannah said. The top floor appeared to be closed to the public—probably office or event space.

"Let's start at the beginning." Liam led the way into the first gallery.

The walls were hung with a dozen paintings, including several portraits and landscapes. Given the resemblance to the Thomas Cole painting, she guessed these were more from the Hudson River School era. She walked along the gallery, taking in names like George Inness, Thomas Doughty, and Susanna Paine.

"Louis Comfort Tiffany," Lacy said, pointing to a painting of a woman lying on a lounger, reading a book. "He was a painter too?"

"I guess." Hannah wished she knew more about art.

The paintings were beautiful, but what stood out most on the walls were two blank spaces where the shapes of absent paintings had been outlined in black tape. Below the outlines were placards that explained what had happened to the paintings and showed what they had looked like.

"Here's where the Thomas Cole piece was," Lacy said, pointing to one of the outlines.

"And this is that *Peaceable Kingdom* one," Liam said.

"Hopefully those two will be returned to their spaces soon," Lori said.

"I'm sure they will be," Hannah said. "They probably have to check them over for any damage before hanging them up again."

The group wandered into the next gallery and saw the empty space where the Winslow Homer had hung. Upstairs they found the places where the Edward Hopper, Mary Cassatt, John Singer Sargent, Georgia O'Keefe, Andy Warhol, and Roy Lichtenstein paintings had been displayed. The Rothko had been returned to its place on the wall, and its placard detailed its history.

It was amazing to see the museum and get a sense of what the space was like. And it was nice to see so many important works of art, even if Hannah didn't totally understand what made them important. It helped her visualize what had happened here, even if it didn't get her any closer to understanding the details.

There were also more visitors here than she would have expected on a Thursday morning in May. There were at least half a dozen other people in each of the galleries they walked into, which seemed like a decent number, given that this was a small museum in Kentucky rather than one of the large public ones in New York or Washington, DC.

They headed downstairs again, but before they left the museum, Lacy excused herself to use the restroom. "Where I spend most of my time these days," she joked as she headed in. Lori went in as well, but Hannah hovered outside, reading a list of museum supporters printed on the wall by the ticket desk. The Carlyle Foundation was listed near the top, with donors at the highest level.

"Can I help you with anything?" asked the young woman seated at the desk. Her long black hair was pulled into a sleek ponytail, and she blinked owlishly at Hannah from behind oversize glasses. Her name tag read SLOANE.

"Do you know anything about the Carlyle Foundation?"

"I know they're big supporters of the museum," Sloane said. "But that's it. I'm not on the development team. They might know more." Hannah had learned from the podcast that *development* was code for *fundraising*.

"Is anyone on the development team available to speak with today?" Hannah asked.

"Not without an appointment." Sloane reached for a brochure. "Though, if you're interested in making a tax-deductible donation to support the collection, I can give you some information."

"Sure." Hannah knew the museum would be sorely disappointed by the size of the contribution she would be able to make, but she supposed that when it came to funding the arts, every little bit counted.

"What about Montgomery Carlyle?" Hannah asked.

"Who?"

"He was a former board member of the museum," Hannah said.

Sloane shrugged. "I don't know. I've only been here six months. Probably some rich guy, if I had to guess."

"What makes you say that?" Sloane probably wasn't wrong, but Hannah was curious why she thought that.

"His name is Montgomery Carlyle, for one thing," she said. Hannah wanted to laugh, but had to admit she had a point. "But also, that describes pretty much all the board members, past and present."

"He was around when the theft of those paintings happened back in the nineties," Hannah said.

"Definitely an old rich guy, in that case."

Hannah wasn't sure if the woman truly didn't know anything more or didn't want to share, but in any case, she wasn't going to get any more out of Sloane.

"There is a pretty good crowd here," Hannah said.

"Yeah, we usually have a good number, especially since that podcast dropped last year. It's been bonkers since then. And it's been even busier after news broke that two more of the stolen paintings have been found. Did you hear about that?" Sloane asked.

"I did," Hannah said. She decided not to elaborate. Instead, she had another question. "So it's not unusual to have a good number of visitors, then?"

"Not really. Again, this is more than normal, but there's always a crowd here. Vultures, we call them, though I'm probably not supposed to tell you that. They come to see the places where the stolen art used to hang. Most people who come here are more interested in the missing art than the art that's here, truth be told."

"Wait. You're saying people come just to see the missing art?"

Sloane wrinkled her nose. "Totally. We're famous for being the museum with some of the most valuable stolen art in the world. Isn't that how you heard about this place?"

Hannah reluctantly admitted it was. And she realized that she was guilty of being a vulture too.

"In some ways, having that art disappear was the best thing that ever happened to this place," Sloane continued. "I mean, obviously it's terrible too, what with the masterpieces going missing. But also, the museum was in bad shape and probably would have closed or had to sell off its art before the publicity from the theft got people interested in it. Thirty years later, people are still coming to see the missing art. That theft kept us in business."

Hannah wanted to ask more questions, but another woman came out from behind a door and Sloane went back to her computer, making it clear that she wouldn't say anything more. She probably shouldn't have said that much, though Hannah was grateful that she had. It gave her plenty to think about on the drive home.

Margot called on the way back from Frankfort, but Hannah silenced the call. Lacy was telling Lori and Daniel about her monthly puzzle nights, and Hannah didn't want to interrupt the conversation by answering a phone call now. Hannah was grateful to have her chatty friend along. Lori and Lacy were getting along swimmingly, and it allowed Hannah time and space to think.

According to Sloane, the theft had basically saved the museum. Was there any chance someone at the museum had understood human nature and predicted that would happen? Had that been the plan all along, or was the increased foot traffic a happy accident?

After Liam dropped Hannah off at home, she went upstairs and called Margot back. Jacob was already at work inside the Hot Spot, getting things ready for dinner, but she needed to change and run a brush through her hair before heading to work anyway, so she had a few moments to talk.

"Hey," Hannah said when Margot answered the call. "How's it going?"

"Good," Margot said. "I wanted to let you know that I found some information about Dickie McAllister."

There were so many names floating through Hannah's mind that it took her a minute to place that one. "Montgomery Carlyle's friend in the art world, right?"

"Right. The one who had a meteoric rise in the gallery world in the nineties."

"What did you find out?"

"I'm guessing you were looking for a connection to the stolen art, right? Some way of connecting his ascendancy in the New York art world to the museum thefts in Kentucky?"

"If there is one, yes."

"Sorry to disappoint you, but I haven't found one," Margot told her. "What I did find is a stepfather named Benjamin Helmers who owns Helmers and Grant Galleries. They're based in Switzerland, and they're one of the biggest and most important galleries in the world. I didn't make the connection at first because the last name is different, but I did some digging. It seems like Dickie's rise has more to do with a very rich, very powerful stepdad than any connection to Montgomery Carlyle."

"Well, that's too bad."

"In that it means there's no clear connection to help you solve your mystery, sure. In the larger sense, though, I mean, maybe it's not so bad that he didn't get where he is by fencing stolen art."

"Of course." She felt silly now. Margot was right, obviously. "I'm glad to hear he got his position the old-fashioned way."

"Nepotism. Exactly," Margot said with a laugh. "Sorry about that."

"No, thank you for looking into it for me," Hannah said.

"There's one more thing I thought of, and I wanted to run it past you, even though it's probably nothing," Margot said. Hannah could hear the screech of seagulls and the sound of crashing waves in the background. Margot was probably walking along the beach, as she did most mornings. For a moment, Hannah had a pang of longing for the beach and the California sunshine. As much as she loved it here, those aspects had been hard to give up.

"What is it?"

"Kingfisher."

"Okay. That was the name of the gallery that sold the Rothko, right?"

"Exactly. It's also the name of one of Vincent Van Gogh's most famous paintings."

"It is?"

"Look it up."

Hannah typed the name into her laptop and saw a picture of a bird on a small branch in front of a pond. "This is the same guy who painted *Starry Night* and all those sunflowers?"

"That's him. He did more realistic works earlier in his career."

"Okay." Hannah was glad to know this, but unsure what she was supposed to do with the information. "So what does that mean? Isn't Van Gogh Italian?"

"Dutch, actually."

"Oh." She supposed it did sound more like a Dutch name, on second thought. "The Witherspoon Museum only has American art, so I don't see what the connection would be."

"I don't either, truthfully," Margot said. "It may be nothing. But once I noticed it, I had to mention it, in case it meant something to you."

"I'm glad you did," Hannah said. "I'll see if I can find anything. And thanks for the info on Dickie."

"Anytime. Let me know what you find out. I'm dying to know what really happened."

That made two of them.

Hannah spent a few minutes looking through a website that listed most of Van Gogh's paintings in order. She hadn't realized how realistic his early paintings were, or how many of them were ordinary portraits, or landscapes, or still lifes. Or how many of the people in the portraits were dressed so...Dutch. That was a whole lot of bonnets.

She scrolled to the bottom of the page, then back up to study the little bird painting. Was there a clue here? If so, she had no idea what it was.

A text from Lacy came through as she was closing her laptop.

JACKY HOLT CALLED. THEY HAVEN'T BEEN ABLE TO TRACE THE PERSON WHO POSTED THE TOOLS FOR SALE. THEY WERE STILL WORKING ON IT, BUT NO LUCK SO FAR.

Hannah returned to the posting and saw that it was still up. She studied the name of the seller—Jonny Smithers—and the description, looking for any clue that would hint at who had posted it. She couldn't tell much of anything, though. She clicked on the photos of the tools, looking again at the table saw and the toolboxes. They were set out on grass next to what looked like a driveway, and—

Wait.

She had to call Jacky.

Chapter Twenty-Two

"Do you see there, in that third photo?" Hannah said into the phone.

"The one with the table saw that's new in its box?" Jacky said.

"That's the one," Hannah said. "Look in the background."

"Well, I'll be," Jacky said.

"The guy who posted this—"

"We don't know it's a man," Jacky said.

"Okay, well, the person purporting to be Jonny Smithers took a photo of the table saw in the box and didn't notice his truck was in the background."

Hannah had been shocked when she'd noticed the bottom half of a white pickup truck behind the table saw. Sadly, the photo showed the truck from the side, so the license plate wasn't visible, but it was something.

"I'll look into it," Jacky promised. "I have to warn you that half the men in this town drive pickups, though."

"Fair enough. But they're not all white."

"That does limit it some. We'll get to the bottom of it."

It was way past time for her to be downstairs. When Hannah finally made it to the Hot Spot, it was nearly opening time, but when she got in, the dining room was ready to go and the smells from the kitchen told her Jacob had things under control.

Elaine was at the hostess stand with a stack of menus, and Dylan and Raquel were straightening the place settings and filling water pitchers.

"You guys are the best," Hannah said, hanging her bag on a hook in the office. "Thank you."

"We've got everything under control," Raquel said. "You don't need to worry. We know you're busy."

Hannah was glad Raquel was right, because her mind was far away, thinking about everything that had happened in the past few days. Had Geraldine's father, art lover and board member, found a way to save the Witherspoon Museum by arranging for ten of its most important works to be stolen? And was Geraldine responsible for two of those paintings ending up in Lacy's cottage?

Hannah went through the motions, greeting customers, checking on orders, sending a special dessert out for a birthday, but she wasn't present mentally. Which was probably why it took her a while to notice that Elaine was calling her name.

"What's up?" Hannah asked, walking toward her. Two men in dark pants and black T-shirts stood in front of the hostess stand. Both wore sunglasses, even though they were inside the restaurant. One was tall, with a reddish-brown beard, and the other man was shorter, but she could see his muscled arms.

The taller one said, "We're looking for someone by the name of Joanie Gardner."

"Joanie?" Hannah stammered. "She was here yesterday, but why do you ask?"

Joanie went by White now. So why were these men looking for Joanie Gardner?

"We're looking for Joanie," the bearded one said. "Heard a rumor she was in town."

"We heard she was seen here at this restaurant," the shorter one added.

"Like I said, she was here yesterday, but I don't know if she's still in town," Hannah said. "She doesn't live here. I imagine she went back to—I mean, back home." Even if Hannah knew where Joanie was, she would not tell these men, who were clearly trying to intimidate her. Besides, it wasn't her place to hand out other people's contact information, especially to complete strangers.

"She didn't," the younger one said simply.

"Well, I don't know how to help you in that case. I'm sorry about that."

She was relieved when the shorter one nodded.

"Come on," he said. "Let's go."

Hannah watched as they walked out of the restaurant and down the street.

"What was that?" Elaine asked. "Who is Joanie?"

"They were looking for the woman who was here with Christine yesterday," Hannah said.

"Why?"

"I don't know."

"Do you think you should tell the police? Or Joanie?"

Hannah wasn't sure. The men hadn't done anything illegal. She didn't want to report people to the police because she had taken an instant dislike to them. But at the same time, she didn't get the impression they were looking for Joanie so they could have a nice friendly chat with her. She weighed what to do.

"I'll call Christine," Hannah said. She could call Joanie directly, since she had her number, but she decided it made more sense to start with Christine. Hannah didn't want to alarm Joanie unnecessarily, and sensible Christine would know what to do. Hannah went into the office and took out her phone.

"Do you know why two men would show up at my restaurant looking for Joanie?" she asked when Christine picked up.

"What?" Christine sounded startled. Understandably, since Hannah had skipped the niceties. But the situation felt too urgent for small talk.

"There were two men who looked like they spend too much time in the gym here, asking for Joanie."

"What did they want with her?"

"They didn't say, but I didn't get a good impression of them," Hannah said, hoping she didn't sound like too much of an alarmist.

"Joanie went home after dinner last night. She was just in town for dinner."

"They seemed to think she was still in Blackberry Valley."

"That's absurd. Why would she be here? And why would they care?" Christine was asking all the questions in Hannah's mind.

"I don't know."

"I'm calling her right now. Maybe she'll have an idea. At least she should know they're looking for her."

"Let me know what she says."

"Will do," Christine assured her.

Hannah put her phone away and went back out to the dining room, and she jumped in to bus tables when Dylan got behind and loaded the dishwasher when they needed more bowls. But she didn't stop thinking about those men, why they'd been here, and what it meant.

Christine texted her a little while later to say that Joanie was home in Lexington. She didn't know who those men were or why they were looking for her. Somehow, that didn't ease Hannah's mind.

Something didn't add up.

Chapter Twenty-Three

L acy called Hannah first thing Friday morning. Well, first thing
for Hannah. Lacy rose with the sun, but Hannah was nursing her
first cup of coffee when her phone lit up with her best friend's name.

"He came back."

"Who did?" Hannah's brain was still sluggish.

"The tool thief," Lacy said. "He came back again last night, and
we caught him on that camera Neil set up. You can see him on the
video. He drives a white truck and—"

"I knew it!" Hannah interrupted.

"What?"

Hannah explained the truck connection.

"That's amazing," Lacy said. "Anyway, on the video, he tries to
get in through the door but we've got a dead bolt on that now, and
then he goes to the front window again, but it's boarded up with
plywood and he can't get in. There's nothing in the cabin to steal
anyway, because Gus isn't dumb enough to leave his tools there
again, but we caught the culprit on video!"

"Can you see who it is?"

"No, unfortunately."

"Any clues at all?"

"None that I can see. But Neil sent the footage to Jacky. And if
you want to take a look, you can."

"Can you send it to me?"

"Of course."

"Awesome." Hannah took another long gulp of coffee. "How did demolition go yesterday?"

"Good. They got most of the kitchen opened up, and they'll be working on the bathroom today. Gus says we can probably start framing out the new walls by Monday."

"I'm so glad." And Hannah meant it.

"There's still a long way to go. Let's hope the little one cooperates. Oh, it looks like Jacky is calling me back. Let me grab this."

"Talk to you later."

Hannah hung up and finished her coffee. After some oatmeal with slivered almonds and dried cranberries, she got up and started getting ready for her day. She had tons of work to do in the office, but she had already decided she needed to do something else first.

She wanted to do more research into Joanie White. Those men who had been looking for her last night had set off alarm bells. Hannah didn't know why they had been looking for Joanie, but something wasn't right. The lighthearted, outgoing woman she'd met should not have thugs like those lurking around town searching for her. Hannah had realized at some point in the middle of the night that she hadn't really looked into Joanie thoroughly, and only knew what Christine and Joanie had told her. She would head to the library and do a deep dive into who Joanie was, and what connections she had, and—

Her phone rang, and a number she didn't recognize flashed on the screen. It was a local number, though, and something told her to pick it up.

"Hello?"

"Hannah?"

"Yes, this is Hannah." She knew this voice. How did she know this voice?

"This is Geraldine Steele. I was wondering if you had any time this morning to meet up with me. I—" Her voice faltered, but then she continued. "I think there are some things I need to tell you."

Half an hour later, Hannah heard a knock on her apartment door.

"Thank you for meeting me," Geraldine said.

"Of course." She led Geraldine into the living room, and gestured for her to sit on the couch.

Hannah sat down on the other end and turned toward her. Seeing Geraldine here now, wearing what looked like a cashmere shawl and diamond studs in her ears, she felt suddenly self-conscious about her jeans and sweatshirt.

"I'm eager to talk to you," Hannah said, as much to get her mind off the differences between them as to get the conversation going.

"I know." The light caught on the large diamond on Geraldine's finger, casting tiny prisms on the walls and floor. "I'm sorry I was so short when you and Liam came to the gallery. I knew why you were there, and I really did want to talk to you."

Hannah nodded to encourage her to go on.

"I know you went to the Witherspoon Museum yesterday and were asking questions about my father," Geraldine said.

Hannah tried not to show her surprise. Was she being followed? Was Colin surveilling her?

"Mimi, who manages the front desk, is an old friend," Geraldine said by way of explanation. That must have been the person who had come in from the rear while she'd been chatting with Sloane. The woman whose appearance had made Sloane clam up so quickly.

"But how did she know who I was?" Hannah said.

"She recognized Lacy from the newspaper article earlier this week. When she told me a blond woman, a hunky guy, and his parents were there along with Lacy, it wasn't hard to figure out who it was."

"That's some good sleuthing." Hannah had to admit she was impressed.

"Mimi said you were asking questions that made it clear you had doubts about my father's integrity."

"I don't—" Hannah started, but Geraldine cut her off.

"I know how it looks, with Colin and I having lived in that cottage," Geraldine said. "But we don't know anything about those paintings. If they were there when we lived there, we didn't know anything about it. I wish I had. If I could have returned those paintings to my father, it would have been the greatest gift I could have given him. He never stopped thinking about those paintings, wishing he could track them down. Their loss haunted him."

This was the second person who had allegedly been haunted by the art theft, but Hannah suspected this was a very different scenario.

"What do you mean?" she asked.

"I know what people said," Geraldine explained. "I heard the rumors that it was an inside job, that the museum needed the money and faked the theft for the insurance, or to sell the paintings on the black market. That my dad's business was in trouble and then things turned around at just the right time. That part is true, but it was totally unrelated to the museum theft. I guess the rumors were inevitable, really. People are always going to assume the worst, aren't they?"

"So there wasn't any truth to them?"

"Not at all," Geraldine insisted. "What kind of art museum would set up a fake robbery for ten of the most important works of American art? The whole point of the museum is to preserve the important artwork and to make it accessible to everyone. To then steal, lie, and profit off the black-market sale of the art? It goes against everything the institution was set up to do. Everything Thomas Witherspoon believed in."

When she said it like that, it was a compelling argument. But was it true?

"Frankly, it goes against everything my father believed in too," Geraldine continued. "He loved art. He was a businessman because he had to be, but art was what made him happy. We were always alike in that way. It was what he cared about. Why else would he spend his time and his money on the board of a museum when there were so many other things to occupy both?"

"I guess I don't really know why anyone joins a board."

"You wouldn't do it unless you truly cared about a cause," Geraldine told her. "And he truly believed that making artwork available to the public was the greatest good he could do. He would never have been involved in a scheme to steal the art and rob the public of the experience. That's why I had to come forward and talk to you. I can't bear to have my father's name dragged through the mud."

Hannah appreciated her sincerity. Geraldine genuinely believed her father was innocent. But was she right?

"I've heard that the museum was in financial trouble before the theft," Hannah said. "And that they faced having to sell some artwork before it occurred."

"It may have been true that they were in bad financial straits then," Geraldine said. "I don't really know. I just know that through the years, my father and the trust he set up have always made sure the museum was able to meet its budget. It wouldn't have had to sell anything as long as my father was around. And, by the way, he wasn't around."

"What do you mean?"

"Here." Geraldine reached down into the purse at her feet and pulled out a stack of photographs. She held them out to Hannah. "We were in Italy at the time of the theft. See?"

Hannah saw a picture of a much-younger Geraldine standing beside the man she'd seen in the newspaper articles, and a beautiful woman. The three of them stood in front of the Trevi Fountain. A date stamped in the corner said February 23, 1990. She'd forgotten how old cameras had sometimes added the date to prints. It kind of ruined the photo in Hannah's opinion, but it was useful now. The picture had been taken the day before the theft.

"I remember when my father heard about it. We had just gotten back to our hotel after a tour of the Vatican, and there was a message for him. He crumbled when he heard the news, and spent the next few days distraught, unable to eat or leave the room. We ended up cutting the trip short because he was so upset."

Hannah flipped through the other photos and saw the family posed in front of St. Peter's Basilica and the Colosseum the day of the theft. It really seemed like Montgomery Carlyle had been out of the country at the time of the heist. But Hannah still had some questions.

"How did you and Colin end up living in the cottage on Bluegrass Hollow Farm?" Judging by the size of Geraldine's diamonds and her European vacations, not to mention the money her father apparently donated, the Steeles could have afforded to live somewhere fancier.

"Colin and I met at a party when he was still in the police academy. A friend of mine brought him as her date, and we spent the whole night talking. He asked if he could take me out at the end of it."

"I hope your friend was okay with that."

"She was mad for a while, but she got over it when she met her husband," Geraldine said. "I felt terrible, but you can't control who you fall in love with, right? As much as my father would have liked me to."

"Your father didn't like Colin?"

"He liked Colin well enough. It was the fact that Colin didn't come from our social crowd that he didn't like. He had his heart set on my marrying this state senator's son and, I don't know, heading up the Junior League in Frankfort or something. But I was in love and would only have Colin. Dad eventually came around, because how could you not love Colin? But my marriage to a lowly grunt at the police academy was not what he'd had in mind."

"Colin has done well since then."

"Colin is smart and works hard," Geraldine said with a smile. "Dad would have been proud to see him sworn in as sheriff. But those early years were certainly an adjustment. Colin refused to use the money from my trust to pay for our living expenses, and he insisted we had to make it on our own. There wasn't a lot to make it on, though. You asked how we ended up at the cottage. It's because it was all we could afford."

When she said it like that—unvarnished, upfront—Hannah believed her.

"Like I said, I know it looks bad now, since the art was found in that cottage and with my connection to the museum. But I had no idea it was there. I wish I had. It would have made Dad so happy to return even two of the paintings to the museum. But I truly don't know anything more."

Unfortunately, the fact that Montgomery had been out of the country at the time of the theft didn't mean he wasn't involved. Obviously, he wouldn't have committed the crime himself, even if he'd been behind it. That wasn't him on the security camera footage raiding the museum. He could have set things up and left the country to give himself an alibi. And obviously his daughter thought he was innocent, that he would never have done such a thing. But there was no evidence. None of this proved anything, really.

And yet, Hannah got the sense Geraldine was telling the truth. Everything that had pointed to Montgomery and Geraldine being behind the theft could be explained. It wasn't proof, but she was pretty sure that if Montgomery had been behind the theft, his daughter didn't know about it.

"So who do you think stole the paintings?" Hannah asked.

"Sometimes the most obvious answer is the right one," Geraldine said. "The police have always thought organized crime was behind it."

"And you do too?"

Geraldine shrugged. "Who else could have pulled off such a brazen crime? And who else would have gotten away with it? Tell me, really, who else could it have been?"

Hannah thought about her words all afternoon.

Chapter Twenty-Four

Hannah was still thinking about Geraldine's suspicion that organized crime was behind the thefts as she processed invoices and accepted deliveries that afternoon. She helped get the dining room ready for dinner on autopilot and mechanically comforted Raquel when the waitress was frustrated that she couldn't get in touch with Marshall.

Liam dropped off the painting he'd bought for his mom so he could surprise her with it at dinner that night. Hannah set the painting in her office, but she was still distracted by Geraldine's accusation.

Lacy texted that she had emailed over the footage from the trail camera outside the cottage. SORRY IT TOOK SO LONG, Lacy added. HENNIFER WANTED TO SNUGGLE.

Hannah tried not to think too hard about the claim that one of Lacy's chickens wanted to snuggle with her. She went back into the office, found Lacy's email with a link to the video footage, and eagerly opened it.

The very front of a white pickup truck appeared on screen first, though she couldn't make out the license plate. Then a man walked into view of the camera, wearing a dark sweatshirt and a baseball cap. He went up to the cottage door and tried it, then over to the plywood covering the window and attempted to get it open. When neither option worked, he turned around and walked away and out of view of the camera. The footage was grainy and dark, so she couldn't tell a lot from it, but it was something. They had an image of the guy, whoever he was.

She played the video again, looking for any clues. The guy wore sneakers like every other man around here. The pickup wasn't distinctive. She focused on the baseball cap. What was that design? Hannah squinted and recognized the logo on the hat as the *C* of the Cincinnati Reds. There were plenty of Reds fans around here, so that didn't tell her much. The video was too grainy and dark to reveal much of anything.

"Hey, Hannah," Dylan said, poking his head into the office.

She looked up, startled. "Hi, Dylan."

"Jacob wanted me to ask if you had a chance to look at the info he left on your desk about a commercial waffle iron he wants to get."

Hannah riffled through papers and found one with Jacob's distinctive handwriting. "Please tell him not yet, but I'll get to it very soon."

Dylan nodded toward her screen. "What's that?"

"Oh, it's a video I was watching," Hannah said. "It's a trail cam, and it's at night, so it's really hard to make anything out, but I was doing my best."

"Did you try enhancing it?"

"No," Hannah said. "How would I do that?"

"There are all kinds of programs online that can do it. Want me to try?"

"Sure." She scooted her chair over and pulled the spare in front of the computer. Dylan sat down, opened a web browser, and typed in the name of a service Hannah had never heard of before. She watched as he logged in to the site and uploaded the video to the page.

"How do you know how to do this?" Hannah asked.

"My friends and I used to make skateboarding videos all the time in high school. We did this stuff a lot."

Skateboarding? Hannah had no idea Dylan was into that. And it was hard to imagine, given how clumsy he was. Hannah's face must have shown her confusion because Dylan said, "Yeah, I fell a lot." He gave a good-natured smile. "But we had fun."

She watched as he used different functions and filters to enhance the video. After a few minutes of tweaking, he said, "That's probably as good as it's going to get."

He pressed play, and the video played again, but this time the images were crisper and much easier to make out. There was the guy coming down the driveway from the bottom of the screen. There he was trying to get in the front door. There was his back as he tried to get the plywood off the front window—

"Wait."

Dylan paused the video.

"Do you see that?" Hannah pointed at the back of the man's sweatshirt. Before, it had just been a blurry black swath, but now Hannah could see that there was something on it.

"Oh, wow. Is that—"

"I think it is," Hannah said. "I need to call the police."

Twenty minutes later, Hannah had spoken to Jacky Holt again and forwarded the enhanced video, and Jacky promised she was on her way to investigate right away.

"I'm going to resist putting on my siren, because I don't want to announce that the cops are on their way," Jacky said. "But Alex and I are headed over there right now."

Hannah also sent the video to Lacy, who called moments later.

"It's the Solis Hardware store logo," Lacy said. "Why is the thief wearing a hoodie from our local hardware store?"

"I don't know. But Jacky and Alex are looking into it."

Hannah tried to be present once they opened the doors and started seating customers. She hugged Liam and his parents as they came in, and led them to a table by the window. The whole time, though, her mind was spinning, trying to make sense of the clues. Like one of Lacy's puzzles, she kept trying to fit the pieces together but the complete image refused to form.

Just after the first seating, Hannah came across Raquel standing at the rear of the dining room, typing on her phone.

"I'm so sorry," Raquel said, slipping the phone into her pocket. The staff tried to avoid having their phones out around the customers.

"Is everything all right?" Hannah knew Raquel wouldn't have broken the unspoken rule unless it was important.

"I still can't get ahold of Marshall. We're trying to plan dates for me to take a trip out to see him, and he's not responding. He hasn't for hours."

"That happens sometimes, doesn't it?" Hannah remembered a time a few months back when Marshall had gone silent while on deadline, Raquel had been worried, but all was well.

"Yes, unfortunately." Raquel sighed. "I hate this long-distance thing. I mean, it's worth it, of course. But I'm so tired of it."

"I'm sure he'll get in touch with you as soon as he can."

Raquel grimaced. "Let's hope so."

Liam signaled to Hannah, and she knew it was time. She went to the office and brought out the painting, which he had wrapped in floral paper.

"Happy birthday, Mom," Liam said, handing the package to her.

"You didn't need to get me anything," Lori protested, even as she carefully removed the paper. She gasped at the sight of the painting. "It's beautiful." She held it out and studied it.

"Geraldine Steele painted it."

"I thought it looked like her work. I've always wanted one of her pieces." She gazed at it a few moments more. "It's Sycamore Trail, isn't it? The one we just hiked."

"It is."

"I love it." She handed the painting to Daniel and threw her arms around Liam. "That was so thoughtful of you."

"Hannah helped pick it out," Liam said.

Lori gave Hannah an enthusiastic hug. "Thank you."

She spent a few minutes gushing over the painting, then Hannah brought out a flourless chocolate torte with a candle and they sang "Happy Birthday." People from all over the restaurant joined in. Lori had tears in her eyes, and she kept smiling at Hannah.

Later, Lori found Hannah at the rear of the dining room.

"I wanted to say thank you," Lori said. "Not just for the painting, but for everything. For loving Liam so well. For—well, for being you."

Hannah returned the bright smile. "I do love Liam. I think he's the most incredible person."

"He is," Lori acknowledged. "But so are you. I've been praying for Liam to find a wonderful woman to spend his life with. I've been praying that she would be kind, strong, resourceful, and loving. I've been praying that she would love the Lord and draw my son closer to God. I can't get over how the Lord answered every part of my prayer. We couldn't be happier to have you joining our family. I can't wait for this wedding." She wrapped her arms around Hannah.

All Hannah could do was hug her back and try not to cry.

She expected the Bertholds to head out after that, but after a few minutes of awkward hovering, Daniel approached her. "Thank you," he said. "For everything."

"Thank you," she replied. She didn't know what he was thanking her for, but she went along with it.

"I know I'm not always good with words," he continued. "And Lori tells me I'm too quiet, that I need to show my feelings more. So I thought I should come back here and tell you how happy I am that you and Liam are getting married. You're maybe not exactly who I would have picked out for him—"

What? She tried not to the let the hurt show on her face.

She must not have succeeded, because he immediately said, "I didn't mean it like that. There I go, messing it up again. What I was trying to say was that I thought he would need to find someone exactly like him, someone who loved the things he loves, but I was wrong. What he needed was someone who complements and challenges him. Who makes him a better version of himself. And that's you. I'm trying to say that I am glad Liam chose you, that his wisdom was greater than mine."

It may not have been exactly how Hannah would have wanted it phrased, but it was what she had hoped to hear from him—approval and acceptance.

"Thank you for raising such a good man," Hannah said.

She thought he might try to give her a hug like Lori had, but Daniel stood there awkwardly and nodded. "Well, have a good night," he said, and turned around to rejoin the group.

Hannah had to smile. Liam's father may not be the smoothest talker, but he was a good guy and he liked her. She would take that as a victory.

As Hannah and her crew were cleaning up, someone knocked on the front door. Hannah went to unlock it to tell the customer they were closed, but when she got there, she saw that it was Marshall Fredericks.

"Hi, Hannah," he said. "Is Raquel here?"

That was why he'd been unavailable. He'd been driving to Blackberry Valley.

"She sure is." Hannah stepped aside and let him in, and he walked into the dining room and looked around.

He spotted Raquel about the same time she turned and saw him. Her hand flew to her mouth. "Marshall! What are you doing here?"

Marshall walked toward her in long strides. "Hi, Raquel. I wanted to tell you how much I hate being apart from you."

"I hate it too," Raquel said. "That's why I was trying to find a date when I could come see you."

"A visit here and there isn't enough," Marshall said firmly. "I realized that as much as I love my job, I hate being apart from you more."

Hannah felt kind of awkward watching the drama unfold, but there wasn't really anywhere to go to give them privacy. He was doing this right in the middle of the dining room. Elaine and Dylan were also there, and none of them seemed to know what to do.

"So I wanted to let you know I quit," Marshall continued.

"You *quit?*" Raquel echoed, as if the word made no sense to her.

"I put in my notice today, then I got in the car and drove all the way here to tell you. I'm moving home. For good."

"You are?"

"I am." He stepped forward and kissed her. Hannah ushered Elaine and Dylan into the kitchen. Nothing needed to be done in there, but she'd give Raquel and Marshall a few minutes to themselves.

When she finally got home to her apartment, Hannah was tired and happy, but she was anxious too. With all that had happened that evening and all that swirled around in her mind, she knew she wouldn't be able to get to sleep any time soon. She pulled out the piece of paper where she'd made notes about the case before and began writing down everything that was in her head.

Albert, Nicole, and Joanie had all been crossed off the list as suspects. Geraldine too, honestly, which didn't leave her with a lot. George Fowler and Mark Hillyer had lived in the cottage, but they had both passed away. Geraldine thought organized crime was behind the theft, and if she was right, that gave credence to the rumors that Vinnie Amelio was responsible. It didn't seem nearly as far-fetched now as it had when she'd first heard the idea, but she didn't have any clue what to do about it. For more than thirty years the police had been unable to pin the theft on him. She didn't see how she would be able to do so now, especially if she couldn't talk to him.

She imagined what it would be like to have a conversation with the renowned mobster. Would he be handcuffed and wearing orange? Would they have to talk through plate glass using little phones? She had to laugh at the image, and then at her own hubris, thinking she might get him to confess when no one else had. It was silly to imagine she could. If Vinnie was behind the theft, they might never know what really happened.

Her mind landed on another piece that didn't seem to fit, trying to figure out where it went. Those men who had been looking for Joanie. Vinnie was in jail, but surely he still knew people on the outside. Those guys hadn't looked like mobsters to Hannah, but then again, she had never met one in real life. She realized her mental picture of organized crime was straight out of the 1920s. Maybe not all Mafia dons wore fedoras these days. Was there any chance those guys were working for Vinnie Amelio? Why had they been looking for Joanie? How could Joanie—sweet, funny, librarian Joanie, who had changed her surname—be involved in all this?

Joanie had lived in the cottage, and not long after the theft, Hannah reminded herself. Joanie had had the opportunity. And even if there hadn't been any work done on the house while she lived there, she had grown up around construction. She knew her way around tools, Christine had said. Did she know her way around dry-wall too? Could Joanie have taken down that part of the wall, put the paintings inside, and sealed it back up so no one would ever know?

But even if she had, how could she be connected to Vinnie?

Hannah mulled over everything Joanie had told her, and everything Christine had told her about Joanie, and something else stood out. Joanie had moved into the cottage because she'd just divorced her husband.

What about the ex-husband? Hannah didn't know anything about the guy, not even his name.

She opened up her laptop and searched the name *Joanie White*, then the name *Joanie Gardner*. She saw all the same things she'd found before, which was pretty much nothing. How had Joanie managed to stay off the internet so completely? It was almost eerie. As if she had paid someone to wipe the search results, or simply worked very hard to stay away from anything that would get her mentioned online. There was certainly no mention of a husband. It wasn't so surprising that she wouldn't post about a man she'd divorced more than thirty years ago, if her own name didn't turn up anything. But who was he?

Christine would probably know the ex-husband's name. She'd gone to the wedding. But it was after eleven and Christine would be asleep by now, so Hannah couldn't call her. But there was another way she could find out. Joanie was from Louisville, which was in Jefferson County.

Hannah opened the website for the county's vital records and did a search for the name *Joanie Gardner*. There was a birth certificate. She felt almost triumphant. Finally, proof that Joanie Gardner existed.

The next link led to a record of marriage between Joanie Gardner and Beckett Harmsworth in 1987. That was the ex, then.

According to this, Joanie had changed her name to Harmsworth. When did it change to White? Had she gotten remarried at some point? If she had, she hadn't mentioned that, and it must not have been in Jefferson County as there was no record of it.

Beckett Harmsworth.

Where had she heard that name before? It was unusual enough that it stuck in her mind, and she knew she'd heard it recently. Or maybe she'd read it. But where?

Hannah racked her brain, but couldn't come up with anything. And that was the only record in Jefferson County. But there was a link at the top of the page that indicated there was a way to access records from all over the state of Kentucky. She clicked on that and did a search for *Joanie Harmsworth*.

Well, this was interesting. Joanie and Beckett Harmsworth had bought a house together in Frankfort, Kentucky. Joanie had never mentioned that she'd lived in Frankfort, even when Hannah told her about the theft at the museum in the same town. Was that just an oversight? Or had she had a reason to keep that fact quiet?

Hannah kept looking. That was the only record for the name *Joanie Harmsworth*. And she didn't find anything else for the name *Joanie Gardner*. But when Hannah typed in the name *Joanie White*, something interesting came up. There was a property record. Hannah clicked on the link and squinted at the address.

It was for a place in Chester, Kentucky. Hannah researched the address and saw that it was a cabin right on a body of water called Spring Lake. That must be the place she had been talking about at dinner with Christine. But she'd talked about it as her grandparents' cabin, and Hannah had gotten the impression that it was no longer in the family. Had Joanie actually said so? Hannah replayed what she could remember of the conversation and realized she probably hadn't, but Hannah had assumed that was what she meant.

Regardless, the cabin was very much still in the family, and in fact had been inherited by Joanie herself. Joanie definitely hadn't mentioned that part—but why not? Was it a purposeful omission, or just something she had decided not to bother to spell out?

The cabin was cute, at least from what Hannah could tell online, which wasn't a lot. And the property record showed that it had been transferred to Joanie by the estate of Edward P. Gardner. She jotted down the address and kept looking, but didn't see anything.

Back to figuring out how she knew the name Beckett Harmsworth. Hannah thought back through everything she'd read in the past few days. She'd talked to a lot of people and read so many things. Beckett wasn't on the list of names of people connected with the cottage. She did a search and reread the articles she'd seen about the theft, but there was no Beckett there. Had the name been mentioned on *A Brush with Danger*? No, she'd read it somewhere.

Grabbing her phone, Hannah opened the files of documents from Albert's lawyer. She thumbed through the sections, keeping her eyes peeled.

There. Beckett Harmsworth was on the list of people the police had interviewed about the theft, right alongside Vinnie Amelio.

Hannah felt her heartbeat speed up.

Why had Joanie's husband been interviewed along with the infamous Vinnie Amelio?

She went to her computer and typed in the name *Beckett Harmsworth*. A number of articles came up right away from the *Newport Times*.

MAN WITH SUSPECTED MAFIA TIES ARRESTED IN IMPORTING SCHEME

MOBSTER ARRESTED FOR HEADING SMUGGLING RING

ORGANIZED CRIME IS ALIVE AND WELL IN KENTUCKY

Beckett's name was coming up with ties to organized crime.

The puzzle pieces were starting to fit together.

Hannah read the articles and quickly discerned that Beckett had owned a shipping company that moved goods all over Kentucky and beyond. But from what she could tell from these articles, it wasn't always legitimate goods that were being shipped. Sometimes, it seemed, items needed to move from state to state without being noticed, or even disappear completely, and Beckett was able to help.

Which led to the obvious question: Could Beckett have been involved in making the paintings disappear?

But the most startling article was the one she clicked on next:

MOBSTER DEAD IN APPARENT ACCIDENT,
POLICE INVESTIGATING
April 2, 1990
Police in Newport are investigating the death of Tristate Shipping owner Beckett Harmsworth, who was killed in a car accident Saturday on the Roebling Bridge. The accident occurred at 2:41 a.m., when Harmsworth's car spun, slid into oncoming traffic, and slammed into one of the bridge's towers.

Investigators are looking into what caused Harmsworth's car to spin. In a press conference, police chief Matthew Gaither called the circumstances "suspicious." Gaither refused to elaborate on why or what he thought happened, but he did say that the incident would be thoroughly investigated.

Harmsworth was suspected of having connections to organized crime boss Vincent Amelio. His company, which employs a fleet of trucks to move goods around the country, has been investigated a number of times, and Harmsworth has faced prosecution for illegal activities. An anonymous source reports that Harmsworth was being investigated for his possible role in the theft of ten valuable works of art from the Witherspoon Museum in February of this year.

Hannah read the article through again, then sat back in her chair. Several pieces of the puzzle slid neatly into place. If any of this was true, it changed everything.

She needed to call Christine. She needed to talk to Lacy. But by this time, it was almost eleven thirty. Far too late to call them. Even Liam, whose irregular work hours meant he was often awake at odd times, would probably be asleep. She texted him anyway, just in case.

Her adrenaline was pumping, and she knew that even if she couldn't talk to anyone, she still wouldn't be able to sleep. Her mind was filled with scenarios and possibilities, and she had no way to prove any of them.

There was one piece of the puzzle that didn't fit, though. If she was right, she had an idea how those two paintings ended up in the cottage. And she thought she understood the dire consequences for Beckett of two paintings from the heist going missing. She even understood why Colin had warned her to stay out of this—there were dangerous people involved. Beckett's suspicious death made that abundantly clear. There was one more thing she didn't understand.

But she had an idea of how she could figure it out.

Chapter Twenty-Five

The sun had barely come up when Hannah called Lacy, after a night of precious little sleep. "We need to talk to your mom."

"A very good morning to you as well," Lacy said, laughing.

Hannah was not to be sidetracked. "Sorry. Good morning. And also, I need to talk to your mom right away."

"Why? What did you find out?"

"I'll explain soon. But first there's something at the cottage I want to look at. Can you call your mom and ask her to meet us there?"

Lacy must have understood that this was important, because she didn't ask any more questions. "I'll let you know when I get ahold of her."

A few minutes later, Lacy texted to say that Christine would meet them both at the cottage in an hour. Hannah texted Liam to see if he was awake. When he replied right away, she let him know that she'd figured some things out and would be meeting Lacy and Christine at the cottage. Then he texted back immediately that he would join them.

Don't you need to take your parents to the airport? she asked.

Not for several hours. I wouldn't miss this. See you soon.

Hannah got dressed and spent some time reading her Bible, though she had trouble focusing because she was too excited. She got in her car well before she needed to leave and made a stop at Jump Start to get coffee for them all before she headed out to the farm. Not that she needed the caffeine. She was wide awake.

As she drove, the rolling hills flying by, Hannah got a call from Jacky Holt, which she answered on her hands-free system.

"I wanted to let you know your tip was good," Jacky said. "Well, both of them were, I guess. We went out to Solis Hardware last night and asked Mike Solis which of his employees drives a white truck, and he gave us a name. It didn't take long to find evidence that the pickup driver was our man."

"How?" Hannah asked. "Did he confess?"

"Not exactly," Jacky said. "But a visual check of the pickup gave us what we needed. Didn't even have to get a search warrant to see he was our guy."

Hannah took that to mean he had left the stolen tools in the truck, either in the cab or in the back, where they were visible.

"He's at the station being questioned now, but we already found some extremely interesting evidence on his phone. This might be big."

"What was it? What did you find?"

"Can't tell you that, I'm afraid," Jacky said.

"Can you tell me who the thief was?" Hannah asked.

"I wish I could," Jacky said.

Hannah tried not to be frustrated. She knew she was lucky Jacky had called to tell her this much. Besides, she had put together a few things that she wasn't quite ready to tell Jacky. Not before she talked to Christine, anyway.

"Thank you for letting me know," Hannah said.

"You bet," Jacky said, and hung up.

Hannah arrived at the farm ten minutes early, but still found Lacy and Christine both waiting outside the cottage. Liam pulled in right behind her.

"Hi." Hannah handed out the coffees, including a decaf for Lacy. Liam kissed her cheek as he took his.

"I'm dying to know what you discovered," Lacy said, using a key to unlock the dead bolt on the front door. "Let's go inside so you can spill."

The interior of the cottage had changed a lot since she'd seen it last. The inside walls had all come down and there were new walls framed out with two-by-fours, outlining where the new bathroom and bedrooms would be. The cabinets and appliances were all gone from the kitchen, but some of the old drywall still clung to the inside of the exterior walls. Chunks of drywall and piles of dust littered the ground along the wall. Lacy handed out dust masks.

Hannah went over to where the paintings had been found, hoping to see some indication that her theory was right. This was why she'd wanted to come here this morning, hoping there might still be a clue left in the drywall. She studied what was left of it, but the section that had covered the paintings was gone. She walked up to the wall and peered into the space between the studs. There were also no more paintings. She peeked in the spaces between the drywall and the exterior wall, checking all along the open wall, but she didn't find any evidence that anything else had been hidden there. Some old insulation, some broken plaster, and lots of dust, but no paintings. So that idea was a bust too.

Oh well. That didn't mean her theory was wrong. She just didn't have proof.

"Christine, how did Joanie end up living in this cottage?" Hannah asked.

"I told you, she was going through a divorce and needed a place to stay," Christine said.

"I mean, did she reach out to you to ask about the cottage specifically, or did she let you know she needed a place and you offered it?"

"She showed up at the farm," Christine said. "She said she'd left Beckett and needed to get away from everything for a while to grieve and process. She told me she wanted to go to the most isolated place she could find, and this farm came to mind."

"It was a good thought," Lacy said.

Christine nodded. "I think she really wanted a break from her old life. The cottage happened to be empty at the time. She said it was perfect, and she moved in that day."

"She had her things with her?" Hannah asked.

"She had two big suitcases, as I recall," Christine said.

"That was it?" Liam's eyebrow quirked up. "She was leaving her old life behind, and it all fit into two suitcases?"

"Well, she wasn't moving in permanently, so she didn't bring furniture or anything. Her stay was only meant to be temporary. And the cottage was furnished, so it worked out perfectly."

"Did Joanie ever say anything about not telling anyone she was here? Or act secretive in any way?"

"Hannah, what are you asking?" Lacy demanded, clearly startled.

Christine waved away her daughter's protest. "Hannah's right. She didn't want anyone to know she was here. She said Beckett was very angry about her leaving, and she didn't want him to figure out where she was until she was ready to face him."

"Did she say when that would be?" Hannah lowered her mask and took a long sip of her coffee.

"No, but I also didn't ask." Christine said. "You can't put a time-line on grief."

"Did it feel odd to you that she didn't want anyone to know she was here?" Lacy asked. Hannah thought her best friend was starting to wonder the same thing she was.

"Not at the time," Christine said slowly. "Like I said, she was grieving, and grief can do strange things to people. But now that you're asking about it, I guess I can see that it may have been kind of extreme. She asked me not to tell anyone she was here. She didn't really leave the cottage except to go for walks in the woods. I bought her groceries because she didn't want to go into town. So, yeah, now that I see what you're suggesting, I can understand how maybe I should have asked more questions."

"Joanie didn't come off as the shy, retiring type to me the other night," Hannah said.

"She isn't," Christine agreed. "But she was different at the cottage. She seemed reserved, almost scared. I didn't see it that way at the time, of course; I thought she was simply grieving, like she said. But in retrospect, I can see how she might have been scared."

"How she might have been hiding?" Lacy suggested.

Christine nodded, biting her lower lip.

"Did you ever wonder why she didn't go to her family's cabin on Spring Lake?" Hannah asked. "If she needed a retreat, wouldn't that have been the logical place for her?"

"I—" Christine started, and then faltered. "I guess I didn't. Maybe someone else was using it. Honestly, I never thought to ask. I saw my friend needed help, so I did everything I could to help her."

"Which says a lot about you as a friend," Lacy said, laying a hand on her arm.

"Are you suggesting that Joanie didn't go to her family cabin because she didn't want to be found, and that would have been an obvious place to look for her?" Liam asked Hannah.

"I'm just asking questions and trying to get a full picture of the situation," Hannah said. But Christine's answers were confirming her suspicions. "Do you remember when she moved out of the cottage?"

"I wasn't sure of the timing before, but I looked back at some papers yesterday and she was here from February to April of 1990. So, before George Fowler."

Hannah had guessed as much. "Do you remember exactly when she moved out?"

"Not really." Christine paused a moment. "Wait. I know it was right after my birthday. She refused to come to town to celebrate with me, and I was kind of annoyed. With all I was doing for her, I felt like she could have done this one thing for me, but she wouldn't."

"Mom's birthday is April 8," Lacy said.

Which meant Joanie had left the cottage less than a week after Beckett died under mysterious circumstances. Then changed her name at some point.

"You said you lost touch with her pretty soon after she moved out," Hannah reminded Christine.

"Yes, but again, back then, it was harder to stay in contact. She moved, and I didn't have her new phone number. I was busy running a farm and raising a child. I probably should have tried harder to reach out, but these things happen. People drift apart."

Hannah couldn't argue with that. But it didn't change the strange timing of Joanie's move, or the fact that she'd changed her last name with no apparent explanation. Or that she'd never reached out to the best friend who had helped her in her time of need. Surely Christine didn't need Hannah to point out how odd that was.

"What are you getting at?" Lacy asked her. "I can see that you're suggesting Joanie was the one who brought the paintings to the cottage—"

"In those big old suitcases," Christine added.

"But I don't understand how you got there," Lacy said.

Hannah took a deep breath and explained how the men who'd come to her restaurant had tipped her off that Joanie might be more than she appeared.

"Wait, there were mobsters looking for her?" Christine asked, her eyes wide with alarm.

"I don't know who they were," Hannah said. "But maybe. If she's back on their radar because of the paintings being found, and they somehow knew she'd come to town, it might make sense."

"But why would mobsters be interested in Joanie?" Christine asked.

Hannah explained how she'd found the articles tying Beckett to Vinnie Amelio, and about his being interviewed in connection with the theft.

"Wait. Joanie's husband was actually in the mob?" Lacy asked.

"I don't know for sure, but it seems to be a possibility," Hannah said.

"But Joanie would never marry someone like that," Christine said. "She couldn't have."

"I have no doubt that she would never knowingly marry someone like that," Hannah said. "I'm suggesting that she might not have known. Maybe she believed his shipping company was just that—shipping."

"You said he was handsome and charming," Lacy pointed out to her mother. "Maybe she fell in love and didn't ask too many questions."

Christine was quiet for a moment, obviously considering this option. "It did happen pretty fast. She said it was love at first sight, and when you know, you know."

"You met him, right?" Lacy asked Christine. "Did he come across as a mobster to you?"

"I don't have the first clue what a mobster would be like," Christine said. "So I guess the answer is no."

"We're just speculating here," Hannah reminded them. "But if my assumptions are right, I don't think she understood what he was really doing for money or about his connections. Because it seems like she left him pretty shortly after the museum heist, then hid out here until he died. Which suggests to me that she didn't know, but once she knew, she left him and really didn't want him to find her."

"And she didn't want him to know where she was because she was scared of him and his mobster friends," Christine said, nodding.

"Maybe. Or it could have been because of something else," Lacy added.

"Right," Hannah said. "It could be that she didn't want anyone to know where she was because when she left him, she took a few things with her."

"Some mementos of their time together, you might say." Lacy's mind had gone right where Hannah's had.

"Or as an insurance policy," Hannah added. "To make sure she had the upper hand, or to keep as a nest egg. There are any number of reasons she might have tucked a couple of the paintings Beckett was supposed to fence into her suitcase when she left him."

"You're saying Joanie is our thief," Christine said. "When she left him, she took two of the stolen paintings."

"That's what it looks like," Hannah agreed. "And then she found a place where he wouldn't be able to find her. She stayed out of view and made sure no one knew she was here."

Christine sighed. "So, if you're right, what was her long-term plan? How long did she think she could stay here without being found out?"

"I don't know," Hannah said. "Maybe she didn't know. We'd have to ask her. But I suspect once she heard that Beckett had had an 'accident,' she realized she had to get rid of the paintings."

"You think Beckett was killed because of the missing paintings?" Lacy asked.

"I think it's a possibility," Hannah said. "Those paintings were worth millions. If Beckett was supposed to have them, but Joanie took them and he couldn't find her, the people who were expecting those paintings might not have been too pleased. So when Beckett couldn't produce the paintings, he might have been made to disappear."

"That's dark," Liam said.

"It's the Mafia," Christine said. "I guess that's about what you would expect."

"Beckett's 'accident' would have been Joanie's cue that she should not mess with those people," Lacy said.

"And that Beckett wasn't looking for her anymore," Hannah said. "But she probably knew that the mob might be. So she changed her name and stayed under the radar after that."

"So she got out of here, and she left the paintings behind," Christine said.

"But how did she get them behind that wall?" Lacy asked.

"Her dad was in construction. She knew how to use tools," Hannah reminded her. "My guess is that she bought the materials she needed—maybe she went into town in disguise or something—cut a hole in the drywall, slipped the paintings inside, and closed it back up. With a coat of paint, no one would ever know. I wanted to come here this morning because I was hoping I might be able to see where it had been patched, and that might be proof of some kind, but I see that your demolition crew did a really thorough job of destroying the drywall." She smiled at Liam.

He grinned back.

"Wow." Christine leaned her shoulder against one of the few intact walls as if to steady herself. "I can't believe it. My friend, involved in an art heist."

"We don't know for sure," Hannah said.

"What other explanation is there?" Lacy asked. "Nothing else makes sense."

Hannah had to agree. The pieces all fit.

"Okay then," Christine said. "Let's assume that you're right, and Joanie was the reason the paintings ended up here. What about the tool thefts? If we think those were engineered to stop construction on the cottage to keep the paintings from being discovered, how did she know that we were going to do construction in the first place?"

"That's easy," Lacy said. She unlocked her phone and pulled up a social media app. With a few taps, she found the post where Christine had announced that they were ready to start renovating the cottage.

"Oh." Christine's face fell. "But wait. We're not friends on social media."

"It was a public post," Lacy said. "Anyone can see it."

"Oh," Christine said again. "But why the second break-in? That was after the paintings had been found. What was that for?"

"That was part of why I wanted to come here," Hannah said. "I wondered if there might be another painting, or even more than one, that we hadn't found. That would explain why someone wanted so badly for us not to start construction. But I don't see anything."

"Okay, that part is still a mystery. But we think Joanie saw my post, decided to try to stop the work so the paintings wouldn't be found, and then—what? Hired someone to break in? How do you even do that?"

"I don't know," Hannah said. "That's the part that I haven't figured out yet. But the police have the guy in custody."

"They do?" Lacy exclaimed.

Hannah quickly recounted what Jacky had told her this morning. After she'd finished, there was a beat of silence.

"What is it, Mom?" Lacy said.

Hannah saw that Christine's expression was drawn and sad.

"This is *Joanie* we're talking about," Christine said. "My childhood friend. It's hard enough to believe that she might have had something to do with the painting theft. But hiring someone to break into our house? That's just so hard to imagine."

"It probably seemed better than the alternative," Lacy said. "Having the paintings be found, and having it all come to light. The paintings had been safely tucked away for more than thirty years. She'd gone on and had a happy life." She reached for the edge of the drywall near where she was standing. "Maybe she was worried that if the paintings were found, we'd figure out what had really happened, and the people behind Beckett's death would come after her."

"And it sounds like she might have been right," Liam said.

"But how would the mob—if that's who those men were—have known she was here in Blackberry Valley?" Christine said.

"And why would she come here at all, if she was worried about them finding her?" Lacy asked.

"I don't know," Hannah said. "I suppose those are all questions that need to be answered."

"I guess we need to talk to Joanie," Christine said. She sounded defeated.

"Call her," Lacy suggested. "The sooner we can figure this out, the better."

Christine took out her phone and dialed. But it rang and rang before finally going to voicemail.

"I guess she's busy," Christine said. She left a message asking Joanie to call her when she could.

Before Hannah could think of what to do next, tires crunched on gravel outside. Gus Brody pulled into the driveway and parked behind Liam's Jeep.

"I guess we need to let Colin know about all this," Lacy said.

"He's probably going to be mad that Hannah didn't stay out of the investigation, but he'll be grateful for it when he calms down," Liam added.

"Should we call him now?" Hannah asked. She wasn't particularly eager to have the conversation, but she also knew she couldn't put it off forever.

Gus climbed out of his truck, and his footsteps grew closer as he walked up the path.

"Why don't we clear out of here so Gus and his crew can get to work?" Liam said. "We can call Colin when we get back to town."

That sounded like a reasonable plan to Hannah. She nodded and was about to head for the door when Gus walked in and looked around the kitchen. "What did you all do?"

"What do you mean?" Lacy looked as confused as Hannah felt.

"Who tore apart that wall?" Gus pointed at the spot where the paintings had been discovered.

"He did," Lacy said, pointing at Liam, who had been available to help with more demolition the day before. "With Neil? And the sledgehammers? Remember?"

"They did some of this, but this is all new," Gus said, pointing at the opening. "There was drywall all along here when I left last night."

"I thought this looked like more than what we took down," Liam said, walking forward toward the opening in the drywall. "But I left before you guys, for my mom's birthday dinner, so I figured you just stayed later and did more work."

"It definitely is. It had to be torn out anyway eventually, but I was going to wait until after we got the rest of the room framed,"

Gus said. "All this plaster?" He kicked at the chunks of plaster and dust on the ground. "I would never leave a jobsite like this."

"None of us tore down any drywall," Hannah said.

"The house was locked up when we got here this morning," Lacy said. "And it was like this."

"Well, it wasn't like this when I left last night." Gus looked at the door and ran his hand along the wood, shaking his head. Then he turned and started walking toward the rear of the cottage, probably searching for clues as to what had happened.

Liam nudged at the pile of debris on the ground with the toe of his boot. He kicked over a pile and little clouds of dust rose up.

"What's this?" Liam crouched down next to the pile he'd knocked over and pulled a crumpled piece of paper out of it. He unfolded it, and his eyes widened. "Oh, wow. You guys have to see this."

Chapter Twenty-Six

Liam unfolded the brown paper he'd found and smoothed it out against the floor. "It's like the other ones. The ones we found with the paintings."

Lacy stepped forward. "And what is that?"

Liam reached for what she was pointing at and picked up an index card. "'Cassatt,'" he read.

"Oh my goodness," Hannah murmured. "The Mary Cassatt painting was in here all along."

The Mary Cassatt painting. Hannah had studied the stolen works of art enough to be able to picture it right away. Wide daubs of paint in soft pastel colors formed a mother in Victorian dress, including a wide-brimmed hat trimmed with ribbons and lace, cradling a baby in her arms.

"You mean to tell me that the Mary Cassatt painting was in the wall with the others?" Lacy said. "And we didn't know it?"

"I thought there might have been at least one more," Hannah said. "I was hoping to come here and find it."

"But someone else came and got it first," Liam said, shaking his head.

"Joanie," Christine said quietly.

"It had to be," Hannah added. She remembered the moment during their phone call when she'd told Joanie two paintings had been found in the wall of the cottage. "*Two?*" Joanie had asked. At the time, Hannah had taken it as surprise that there had been more than one. But over the past few days, she'd begun to suspect that Joanie had been surprised to find out they hadn't found all three.

"But how did she get in?" Lacy said. "The door was locked."

"Bedroom window is broken," Gus called from the back of the house. "Whoever it was came in that way."

"We're saying that, after failing to scare us off by hiring someone to break into the cottage and steal tools, and after we found two paintings worth millions of dollars that she left behind here, we think she broke into the cottage to steal another painting worth millions of dollars that we hadn't discovered yet?" Lacy clarified.

"That's what it seems like," Liam said.

"The trail cam should be able to tell you, right?" Hannah pointed out.

"You're right." Lacy pulled out her phone and opened the app. "Hang on." She scrolled through the footage, looking for movement. An awkward pause stretched out, but after what felt like an eternity, she nodded. "Yep. The trail cam picked her up. It was Joanie."

Christine let out a sigh.

"But why would she take it now?" Liam said. "Why at this point?"

"She knew the jig was up," Christine said. "She knew Vinnie's guys were after her because they'd been in the Hot Spot asking Hannah about her. She knew we weren't done with construction and would eventually find the third painting. That her attempts to scare us off hadn't worked."

"*That's* why there was a second break-in after we found the paintings," Lacy said. "It didn't make sense that someone would try to stop us once we'd found the pieces. But there was one more we *hadn't* found yet, and she didn't want us to."

Hannah nodded.

"Okay. So that makes more sense, but Liam's question still stands," Lacy said. "If she left the paintings behind all those years ago, why come for this one now? I thought she wanted to make sure they weren't ever connected to her."

Hannah thought about it for a moment. "I'm sure that was true thirty years ago," she said. "But by this point, she had to know we would put the pieces together—or rather, that someone would. Maybe no one had discovered the connection between her and Vinnie yet, but there was a limited number of people who had access to the cottage. Joanie had to know it was only a matter of time before someone figured it out."

"So she came back, broke in, and took it," Lacy said. "But that still doesn't answer the question of why."

"Maybe as an insurance policy. Maybe because she thought Vinnie's goons wouldn't go after her if she was the only one who knew where the third painting was," Hannah said. "The other two are with the police, so they were never going to get those back, but they had to realize that she knew where the third one was hidden. Maybe she thinks they won't hurt her as long as she's the only one who knows where it is."

"Or maybe she's going to sell it," Christine said. "And get out of here. Flee the country. Start a new life somewhere else."

"I think those are all possibilities," Liam said. "And she is the only one who knows at this point. So I guess the question now is, where is Joanie? Where did she go with the Cassatt painting?"

"No clue," Christine finally said.

But Hannah had another idea.

Chapter Twenty-Seven

They barreled down the highway toward Spring Lake in Liam's Jeep, on the way to the cabin Joanie had inherited. "It's 51 Sunrise Drive," Hannah said, locating the address in her notes.

Lacy reprogrammed the GPS directions on the phone. "Fifteen minutes."

"Let's hope she's there," Christine said. "If she isn't, I really don't know how we'll ever get in touch with her again."

Hannah didn't know whether to hope for that or not, to be honest. She didn't know what they would find, and a small part of her worried that the four of them showing up like this was not the smartest idea. For a moment, she thought about calling Sheriff Steele.

But she decided to wait. What if Joanie wasn't there? Hannah didn't want to call Colin out on a wild-goose chase.

There was no telling if Joanie would talk to them even if she was. And it wasn't like she would endanger her friend. In fact, she was way more likely to talk to Christine than she was to the sheriff. Hannah decided the four of them had a better shot at finding the truth than they would if the sheriff showed up, sirens blaring. They would call him as soon as they learned more.

Chester was a pretty little town surrounded by spruce and poplar trees ten miles off the highway. They passed historic buildings, then fields of corn and wheat and grazing land for animals, before turning onto a dirt road that wound its way lazily around the lake.

"This is familiar," Christine said, taking in the trees that arced over the roadway and the wooden cabins spaced out along the road. "It's farther up, though. Past this bend, there should be a small store that sells ice cream."

Sure enough, they found a small general store with a striped awning. According to the advertisements painted on the windows, they carried a little bit of everything, including ice cream.

"It's just around this next corner," Christine said. "I think."

Bumping over ruts in the dirt road, Liam slowed. Hannah was glad they'd taken his Jeep instead of her Subaru.

"That's it," Christine said, and the GPS confirmed that they had indeed found the right place.

Liam pulled into the driveway, which led under a grove of spruce trees and into a small parking area next to a wooden cabin. The place had two stories, a great view of the lake, a porch, and—oh.

Joanie sat on the porch, watching their approach. She wasn't smiling, but she wasn't frowning either. Hannah tried to read her expression and determine whether she had a weapon of any kind. In this part of the country, it wouldn't be unusual for a firearm to be nearby, and Hannah wondered if they'd made a terrible mistake.

Liam, no doubt also thinking about the possibility that Joanie might have a gun, hopped out and tried to put himself between her and the rest of them, but Christine was already out of the car and hurrying toward her friend. Hannah and Lacy got out too.

"Hello," Joanie said. She stood up and hugged Christine. She didn't have any weapons that Hannah could see. "I was wondering who would find me first—Vinnie's guys, the cops, or you all. I would have put money on it being you, and I'm delighted to see that I was right. That one is sharp as a tack." She nodded at Hannah. "Are the cops on their way too?"

"We haven't called them," Lacy said.

"You probably should," Joanie confessed. "Otherwise they'll think you had something to do with all this. No sense all of you getting in trouble for being the only ones in this entire situation to do the right thing."

Hannah looked at Liam. This was not the reaction she had expected.

"I knew it was only a matter of time before someone found me here," Joanie went on. "I've done a lot of soul-searching over the last few hours, and I've realized that I'm tired of running. I'm tired of hiding. I'm ready to tell them what I know."

"Joanie, we went to the cottage this morning," Christine started. "We discovered that there was a third painting hidden there."

"Yeah, sorry about the broken glass," Joanie said. "I'll pay for it."

Again, this was not what Hannah had been expecting. Joanie, it was clear, was not the hardened criminal the circumstances made her out to be.

"I see," Joanie said, when none of them responded. "You're not sure if you can trust me now. I can understand that. I guess maybe breaking in and taking the painting was a bit dramatic. I thought it was better that way, but now I wish I hadn't. Anyway, why don't you come on in? I can explain everything."

"I'm just going to put in a call to the sheriff first," Liam said.

"Go for it," Joanie said. "Tell Sheriff Steele he was on the right trail and just needed to keep pushing."

Was this a trick? She couldn't really be this calm, could she? She'd finally been found out, all these years later, and she was telling them to call the cops? Hannah was confused.

Liam nodded and pulled out his phone.

"Why are the rest of you standing around down there?" Joanie said. "I'm not going to hurt you. Come inside. You might as well see what you've come all this way for."

Again, Hannah wondered if it was a trick. If going inside would be a mistake. Was Joanie going to tie them up or something? What had they been thinking, coming here without the police?

But Lacy was walking up the steps, and Hannah found herself right behind.

Liam was already talking with Colin on the phone, and he waved to indicate that he would be coming inside shortly.

Hannah was still not sure whether this was a good idea, but she followed her best friend and Lacy's mom into the cabin.

"It's just like I remember," Christine said.

There was a big open space with a kitchen to one side, with dark wooden cabinets and orange vinyl countertops. In front of them, two couches faced each other, and picture windows looked out over the lake. The surface of the water glistened in the bright sunshine.

"If by that you mean that it hasn't been updated in fifty years, you're right," Joanie said with a smile.

To the right of the kitchen was a dining table surrounded by six wooden chairs. And there, in the middle of the table, was the Mary Cassatt painting.

Hannah walked toward it. The photos she'd seen hadn't done it justice. The woman at the center of the picture wore a light lavender gown and a flowered hat. She held the baby with tenderness, even as she gazed off to the side at something off the canvas. It was amazing how the artist had rendered such a touching scene with only tiny dabs of paint.

"So how much have you figured out?" Joanie said.

"Some," Hannah said.

"I bet it's more than some, if you found me here," Joanie said. "What do you want to know?"

"We're pretty sure you hired someone to steal the tools to keep us from doing work on the cottage," Hannah began.

"For all the good it did me. And I'm sorry about that, by the way." She looked at Christine and Lacy as she said this. "It was a terrible thing to do."

"So why did you do it?" Christine asked.

"I thought it would be for the best," Joanie replied. "That we would all be safer—you guys included—if those paintings were never found. I thought I was doing the right thing, though I can see in retrospect that it was kind of pointless. A few missing tools weren't going to stop you. Not with a grandchild on the way."

"But once we found the first two paintings, why did you break in and take this painting, instead of telling us it was there?" Hannah said. "That's what I don't understand. Why, after all this time, would you take this one?"

Joanie didn't answer for a moment. But then she said, "Take a seat, and I'll explain it all."

Liam walked in.

"The cops are on their way?" Joanie asked him.

He nodded.

"Well, I suppose it won't hurt to start without them," Joanie said. She carried the painting to the living area and set it on the coffee table.

They all took seats on the couches, and Joanie started to talk.

"When I met Beckett, I thought he was the most wonderful man in the world. He was smart, handsome, and charming, and he ran a successful shipping business. Big warehouses, lots of trucks coming and going—everything that indicates a business is doing well. He always had plenty of money. I thought I'd won the lottery. Sure, he worked strange hours, but running your own business is hard work. We married quickly, and we were happy. We really were. And I know this sounds crazy, but I need you to believe me: I had no idea. I never would have married him if I'd known what his business actually was."

"When did you figure it out?" Hannah asked.

"When I found five paintings that I'd seen in the news in the back of our closet," she said.

"He kept them in your *closet*?" Lacy repeated.

"He did. I thought mobsters were supposed to be smarter than that. So obviously I confronted him. The museum theft was all over the news. I knew what they were as soon as I saw them, and I couldn't understand why they were in my house. He gave me some story about holding them for a friend, but I knew better. Once I figured out that Beckett was one of the thieves, and that he and his buddy Ricardo had split them up to make it easier to hold them until Vinnie gave them instructions, a lot of things made sense. Snatches of conversations I'd overheard, stories that didn't quite add up, money that seemed to come from nowhere. I couldn't believe I hadn't seen it before. I knew I had to get out of there. I couldn't stay married to a man who'd—I didn't even want to know everything he'd done, to be honest."

"Did you think about alerting the authorities?" Christine asked.

"Of course I did," Joanie said. "Until I found out he'd opened several accounts in my name and had funneled money from his illegal activities into them. I was implicated too. I told him to clear my name or I'd tell the world what he'd done. He convinced me that if I went to the police, I'd spend the rest of my life behind bars. Looking back now, I wish I'd done it anyway. I might have gotten off easy if I'd found a jury that believed me, or I might have gone to jail. Either way, it would have been better than what happened. But I didn't know that then, and I was barely starting out, you know? I didn't want to end up in prison for something I hadn't done. So I left. And I took three of the paintings with me as an insurance policy."

"Insurance against what?" Liam asked.

"I guess I thought that if Beckett came after me, he wouldn't do anything to me as long as I had the paintings. That having them in my possession would keep me safe. It turned out to be the opposite, though. Perhaps if I'd left them where they were, escaped, and told the police what I knew, everything would have been fine."

"When you showed up at the cottage…" Christine started, but didn't seem to know how to finish the sentence.

"I was in a bad way. I needed to disappear. None of what I told you was a lie, Christine. I was grieving the end of my marriage, and I needed a place where I could lay low for a while. All of that was true. Thank you for taking me in and taking care of me. Truly. I've never forgotten your kindness."

"I was glad to do it," Christine said warmly.

"And you stayed there until you learned about Beckett's accident, right?" Hannah said.

"That's right." Joanie closed her eyes briefly. "I never thought they would—I had no idea what they would do to him."

"Was it because he had 'lost' three of the paintings?" Lacy asked.

"I assume so," Joanie said. "I didn't know much about how Vinnie and his men operate. I've learned a lot since then, and I realize I should have known better. But I knew enough at the time to understand that it couldn't have been an accident. That he wouldn't have been allowed to lose three of the paintings and get away with it. I felt terrible. Beckett was mixed up in some shady stuff, no question about it. But he didn't deserve that."

"Did you consider going to the police at that point?" Christine asked.

"Of course I did. But by then I'd been in possession of these stolen paintings for two months, and I knew I had less chance than ever of convincing a jury I was innocent. I also knew that if Vinnie's guys found me, I was in real trouble. Beckett had no doubt told them I had taken the paintings, so I knew they'd be looking for me. I knew I had to get rid of them. So I put them in the only place I could think of where I was sure they wouldn't be found for a long time."

"You did a great job of patching that wall," Christine said. "We never suspected."

Joanie gave her a wry smile. "Dad taught me well. So I left the paintings behind, changed my name, and started a new life."

"I couldn't figure out where the name White came from," Hannah said.

"I just liked it and thought it was generic enough that it would blend in." Joanie shrugged. "I never officially changed it, but it's easy enough to get people to call you what you want. You start using the name, and people don't really question it."

"I tried to get in touch with you a few times over the years," Christine said.

"I know, and I'm sorry about that. I did get the letters you sent to my parents. They never knew the full story, by the way. They knew that I'd divorced Beckett, and I let them believe I just needed to start a new life, but they never really understood why. They wanted me to get remarried and start a family, but I couldn't put anyone else in danger by being associated with me. I felt like there was always a target on my back."

"I can't exactly blame you for that," Hannah said.

"My parents have always been supportive, but they never knew the whole story. I kept my distance from them for their own protection. Anyway, they passed the letters along when I saw them one Christmas. But I couldn't write back. I had already put you in enough danger. I'm sorry, Christine."

"I understand," Christine said. She was either more forgiving or a better actor than Hannah could have been.

"I kept tabs on you, though. I would read the local paper, and I knew what you were up to. I peeked at your social media, once that became a thing. And for a while, things were okay. For a long time, in fact. I was always afraid Vinnie's men would come after me, but then I had a stroke of luck when he was locked up. For a while, it seemed like maybe everyone would just forget about the paintings. Assume they were lost forever. And that worked for over thirty years."

"But then you saw that we were going to do renovations on the cottage," Christine said.

"And you decided to try to stop us," Lacy said. "Why did you hire someone to steal a few tools?"

"It was the best idea I could come up with," Joanie said. "I found him on a message board for the area. I put up a post saying I was looking for help with a special task, and Braden got in touch. Said he lived in the area and could stand to make a few bucks. I don't know why I thought that would work."

"There were lots of things you could have done instead," Liam said. "You could have set fire to the cottage, for one. No one would have found the paintings then."

"Liam!" Hannah protested.

"I'm not saying you should have," Liam added. "Just that you could have covered your tracks that way."

"Liam's a fire chief," Lacy explained. "He's always thinking about fire."

"He's right," Joanie said. "But then the paintings would have been destroyed as well. And as much as I didn't want to get caught with them, I couldn't bear to think of them being ruined."

That was to her credit, at least. She hadn't always made good decisions, but that had been one.

"Plus, I couldn't do that to Christine," Joanie went on. "What I probably should have done was just go in there and take them all out before you started construction. Hindsight, you know. I panicked when I saw that post, so I wasn't thinking clearly."

"But once the two paintings had been found, why didn't you come forward then?" Hannah asked. "When I asked you about them, you pretended you didn't know a thing."

"I suppose a lifetime of pretending is hard to let go of," she said. "I'm sorry, Hannah. I shouldn't have lied to you."

"Why did you come to Blackberry Valley?" Lacy asked. "Was it to see what we knew? Whether we'd figure out about the third painting?"

"Partly," Joanie said. She smiled at Christine. "But mostly it was because I missed my friend. After we chatted on the phone, I wanted to see you again, after all these years."

Christine looked pleased, but Hannah couldn't help but think her pleasure had to be part of a mixed bag of feelings. No matter how true it was that Joanie missed Christine, she'd also had other reasons for coming to see her.

"When did you decide to take the third painting?" Hannah asked.

"The night I came to town. I knew by then that it was only a matter of time before you traced it all back to me, which meant I was in a lot of trouble. And once I realized you hadn't found it yet, but would soon, I decided it would be my insurance policy once again."

"Insurance against what?" Hannah asked.

"My plan was to hide the painting and use it as a bargaining chip when it came to sentencing. I would tell them where it was in exchange for a lesser sentence."

"So why is it here?" Hannah asked. "And not in some bank box somewhere?"

"Because in the end, I couldn't bring myself to do it," Joanie said simply. "I'd forgotten how beautiful it was. How much I loved this painting. It always reminded me of you, you know," she told Christine. "You and Lacy."

"I don't know. I'm not really into hats," Christine joked, and Joanie laughed.

"Anyway, I saw it again, and it made me think if you, and of your little girl about to become a mother herself, and I couldn't do it. I decided I was tired of it all. And I thought about that other one, with all the animals? I loved that one too."

"*Peaceable Kingdom*," Hannah said. "By Edward Hicks."

"I always loved how that one showed how everyone could get along," Joanie said. "Even people who come from totally different viewpoints, totally different likes and dislikes, could let their guard down and try to understand one another. I like to think that that could be true of all humankind someday. And I realized that well, if I really believe that, if I want it to be true, it probably needs to start with me." She gestured at the Cassatt on the coffee table. "Here's the painting, and I'm ready to face whatever consequences are coming my way."

Hannah found herself believing that Joanie was truly at peace with the situation. She supposed that was a good thing, and she hoped that peace held up. She had a feeling Joanie was in for a lot of consequences.

"Do you know what happened to the rest of those paintings?" Liam asked.

"I don't. I assume they were sold on the black market. I would be surprised if they ever resurface, to be honest," Joanie said. "I saw that one they found in New York. That guy must have had a few marbles missing, to display stolen artwork openly like that. Most people are smart enough to hide it or put it in a safe-deposit box somewhere, not show it off. It's a shame, but I truly believe the other pieces are gone for good."

Hannah hoped Joanie was wrong. She hoped somehow the six remaining stolen paintings would be located someday and returned to the Witherspoon Museum collection. She hoped they would again see the light of day. But she was glad that at least this additional one would be put back where it belonged.

They continued asking Joanie questions until Colin arrived, Alex and Jacky on his heels. When Colin walked in, he looked around in confusion at the peaceful scene in front of him.

Joanie stood up. "I'm ready to go. And I'll tell you everything you want to know."

Chapter Twenty-Eight

Colin listened for a few minutes before taking custody of the stolen painting and putting handcuffs on Joanie, who held her hands out willingly. He put her in the back of the squad car and asked them all to report to the station in Blackberry Valley. There, they were questioned separately, and Hannah's interview went on so long her stomach began to growl.

"Tell me again how you made the connection between Vincent Amelio and Joanie," Colin said, flipping to a fresh page of his notepad.

Hannah had already told him once, and she knew the interview was being recorded, but she explained again. She knew Colin was making sure her story stayed consistent, while also giving her the opportunity to relate anything she might have forgotten the first time.

"And you found the cabin where she was staying, how?" he asked.

"It came up in the same vital records search where I found Joanie's marriage license," she answered.

"But how did you know that was where she would go once she'd recovered the third painting? Was that in the vital records file too?"

"No, that was a guess," Hannah said.

Colin gave a tight, grudging smile. Watching him now, seeing how concerned he was to make sure he had all the details right,

Hannah was thankful they had a man like him in Blackberry Valley. He was loyal, dedicated. He had wanted to keep her—to keep them all—safe. This was a man who cared deeply about his town and the people who lived there.

After Hannah had explained every aspect of the story again, he shook his head and gave her another grudging smile. "I thought I told you to stay out of the investigation."

"But aren't you glad I didn't?"

"No, I don't think I'd say that. We would have gotten there."

"Maybe not before a masterwork of American art vanished forever. What's happening with that Braden guy, by the way? The one who took the tools?" Hannah asked because she genuinely wanted to know, but it didn't hurt that her comment also reminded him about her role in that case as well.

"He's been released from custody," Colin said. He hesitated, then seemed to make a decision. "Okay, if you're so smart, then help me understand this. Why exactly did Joanie think hiring him to steal some tools would prevent the paintings from being found?"

"Her logic was pretty flawed," Hannah said. "Obviously a few missing tools wouldn't actually stop the Minyards from working on the house. But I think, when it comes down to it, she thought she was doing something good."

"How so?" Colin tilted his head.

"I can see how, in her mind, Joanie was trying to prevent something bad from happening. If we hadn't found those paintings, none of this would have come to light. Nothing about her past or her ex would have come out. Everything would have gone along peacefully as it had for decades. And she thought that was for the best."

"Three invaluable pieces of art would be lost forever," Colin said.

"I'm not saying what she did was right. I'm just saying that I suspect she did it with good intentions. Maybe go easy on her."

"After she walked off with three masterworks of American art and tried to make sure they never again saw the light of day?" Colin raised an eyebrow.

"There were extenuating circumstances," Hannah said. "And she turned herself in willingly, in the end."

"She didn't turn herself in."

Technically, Hannah supposed he was right. "Okay, fine, but she didn't fight it."

"What I'm trying to say is, I don't know how much grace she can be given. All I can do is present the evidence I've found to the court. It's up to a judge and jury to decide what happens to her."

"What about the Witherspoon? Is there anyone with influence at that esteemed institution who might have some say in what happens to her?" Hannah gave Colin a knowing smile.

He laughed. "I'd be very surprised if Geraldine wants to see the courts go easy on Joanie. But I'll ask."

"It's not like Joanie was the one who broke in and stole the paintings."

"I don't know if the courts or anyone else will see it that way."

He was probably right. No matter how much Hannah understood Joanie's intentions and reasons, it didn't change the fact that she'd had possession of stolen artwork. Instead of returning the paintings, she had hidden them for more than thirty years. Never mind the breaking and entering and whatever other charges came out of the Braden situation. It probably didn't look so good for her.

Finally, after what seemed like hours, Hannah was released to go. She found Liam waiting for her in the lobby.

"Lacy and Christine went home a while ago," he said. "Neil came and got them. Lacy was getting hungry and needed a nap, and I wasn't going to stand between a pregnant woman and her rest."

"You're a wise man."

Liam put his arm around her shoulders as he led her out the door to his Jeep. "You did good work, Hannah Prentiss."

"I had a lot of help."

"I bet it'll be a while before Colin trusts you to stay out of his way, though."

"Maybe he doesn't really want me to stay out of his way. He wouldn't admit it when I talked with him, but I believe he was grateful for what I figured out."

"In any case, maybe for the next little bit, we can focus on something other than solving mysteries."

"Like what?"

"I was thinking perhaps planning a wedding. I can't wait to make you my wife, Hannah." He threaded his fingers through hers as they walked toward his car.

"I'm quite looking forward to that myself," she said.

"Well, you got the hard part over. My parents love you. I knew they would."

"I'm so glad. You have no idea how scared I was."

"Oh, I knew." He grinned at her. "You're not great at hiding it when you're stressed. But I knew you had nothing to worry about. How could they not love you? You're great."

"You're not so bad yourself."

In the quiet that followed, her stomach grumbled. "Sorry."

"I'm starving too," Liam said. "How about we go get some food?"

"What are you thinking?"

"I know a great little place. They serve the best burgers. And I know the owner too. I bet she can get us a good table."

Hannah laughed and followed him to his car. His flattery notwithstanding, she did serve the best burgers in town. And besides, she would follow him anywhere.

She didn't know what the future held, but she knew she would be walking toward it by faith and with Liam at her side, and that was all that mattered.

From the Author

Dear Reader,

Back in the dark days of the COVID-19 pandemic, my kids were doing school on screens and we were camped out at my parents' house in Cape Cod because staying in our apartment in Brooklyn all the time was just too much. We, like most people, watched a lot of TV. Way too much, probably. One night my dad came across a documentary about a theft at an art museum, and since I had nothing better going on, I watched it with him. It ended up being a really interesting series about a brazen art theft at the Isabella Stewart Gardner Museum in Boston, a theft which to this day is unsolved and remains one of the most costly art thefts of all time.

If you've seen that documentary or read about that theft, you probably recognized many elements that came up in this story. In the real theft, thieves dressed like police officers really did tie up the night guard, and then they proceeded to raid the museum and take many of the most important works of art. The thirteen pieces that were stolen—including a Vermeer, several Rembrandts, five Degas drawings, and a Manet—were never recovered. Organized crime was suspected to be involved, but the crime has never been solved.

When I set out to fictionalize that theft for this, I knew I needed to have organized crime as a possible answer to who stole the paintings in this book, but at first that thread seemed really far-fetched.

The idea of organized crime being behind the theft in Boston initially felt a lot more plausible to me than imagining the mob in Kentucky. But when I started looking into a way to make that element believable in this story, I uncovered the history of Newport, Kentucky. Newport truly was the original Sin City, and as I read more, I realized this storyline wasn't as crazy as it first appeared. All the Newport history shared in this story, as strange as it now sounds, is true. If the police hadn't cracked down on the mob in Kentucky, the gambling and other crime that defined Newport probably wouldn't have ever moved out of the state to a little town in the desert called Las Vegas. As they say, truth is stranger than fiction.

While the Gardner Museum featured art from around the world, I knew I wanted to focus on American artists in this book, so I limited the fictional Witherspoon Museum collection to American greats. All the artists in this story are real, and their work can be seen at major museums. I will confess that I don't know a lot about art myself, but my husband is an artist. When I asked him for the names of some American artists whose work might fit well in this book, he immediately suggested Edward Hicks and his series of *Peaceable Kingdom* paintings.

I hope you enjoyed reading this book as much as I enjoyed writing it.

Signed,
Beth Adams

About the Author

Beth Adams lives in Brooklyn, New York, with her husband and two daughters. When she's not writing, she's trying to find time to read mysteries.

The Hot Spotlight

While all of the artists referenced in this book are real, the paintings I've featured in the manuscript are fictional—all except for the Thomas Cole landscape, Picasso's *Kingfisher*, and Edward Hicks's *Peaceable Kingdom* painting.

When I started working on this book, I knew I wanted to feature the *Peaceable Kingdom* paintings because they feel as relevant now as they did when Edward Hicks painted them—more than a hundred versions of the same image!—between 1820 and 1849. Plenty of artists return to favorite subjects. For instance, while I was researching Vincent Van Gogh for this book, I came across dozens of his self-portraits. But it's unusual for an artist to create so many versions of the same painting, each slightly different.

The painting, as Hannah discovered in this book, is based on the messianic prophecy from Isaiah that's quoted in the text. The pictures represent the peaceful coexistence of all creatures. Hicks was a Quaker minister who is said to have painted the work initially to help people visualize the passage. Most of the paintings were initially given away to family and friends. The theme of unity was especially important to Hicks, as the Quaker church was undergoing a schism, and these paintings were reminders that we are all one in Christ.

In a world that seems increasingly fractured, the image of peaceful coexistence through the power of Christ's love seemed like a subject worthy of spending all these pages on.

Today, versions of the painting hang in the Metropolitan Museum of Art in New York, the Pennsylvania Academy of Fine Arts, the Yale University Art Gallery, and many other galleries and museums around the world.

KEY LIME PIE WITH GRAHAM CRACKER CRUST

Ingredients:

For the crust:

½ cup finely ground graham cracker crumbs (blitz in a food processor if you can)

⅓ cup white sugar

6 tablespoons unsalted butter, melted

For the custard:

5 large egg yolks, beaten

1 (14 ounce) can sweetened condensed milk

½ cup key lime juice (or just use regular lime juice—it's still delicious!)

Whipped cream or sliced limes to top, if desired

Directions:

For the crust:

Put all ingredients in a bowl and mix until combined. Press into the bottom and up the sides of a 9-inch pie plate. Set aside until ready to use.

For the custard:

Preheat oven to 375°.

Combine the egg yolks, sweetened condensed milk, and lime juice by hand, in a bowl, or using a mixer. When thoroughly mixed, pour into unbaked crust. Bake until filling is set, about 15 minutes. Allow to cool completely. Top with sliced limes or whipped cream if desired.

Read on for a sneak peek of another exciting book
in the *Mysteries of Blackberry Valley* series!

The Mandolin Mystery

BY CATE NOLAN

Hannah Prentiss looked up as her fiancé, Liam Berthold, entered
Jump Start Coffee on a sunny Friday morning in June. He had
just finished an overnight shift as the chief of the Blackberry Valley
Fire Department. Fatigue weighed on his shoulders, but a smile lit
his face the moment his gaze settled on her. He detoured to greet her
with a kiss before heading to the counter to place his order.

When he returned to the table, coffee and blueberry muffin in
hand, Liam settled into the chair across from her. "You are a sight
for tired eyes. Sorry I'm late."

"Rough night?" Hannah studied the creases etched into his face.
His hair was still damp from the shower he must have taken at the
end of his shift.

Liam nodded. "We were out at the campgrounds for hours after
someone got a little overenthusiastic with a bonfire. It got out of
control pretty quickly. The camp manager was smart enough to call
for help, so damage was minimal. We stuck around to make sure
there was no risk of it reigniting."

Hannah appreciated how conscientious Liam and all the fire-fighters were about protecting Blackberry Valley from fire danger, but she hated the toll it sometimes took on him. "You're free for the rest of the day and have a long nap planned, I hope?"

Liam grinned, and she knew that even though he protested, he loved that she fussed over him. "Yes, ma'am. That's why this is decaf. Unless another emergency arises, I have a date with my pillow. Jealous?" he teased.

Hannah laughed. She loved how easily they joked with each other. It was one of the perks of being great friends as well as being in love.

She sobered. "I hope nothing for the festival was damaged."

Liam gave her a reassuring smile. "No, the campground is set far back from the stage they're building. It was never a threat."

"That's a relief. It would be a shame if the festival had to be canceled, especially because of something like that. I've heard people are coming from all over for it."

Blackberry Valley was set to host the revival of a traditional bluegrass festival in just over a week. The original festival had gone on every year for a decade, until it abruptly ended in the seventies because the founding duo split in an ugly feud. Now the grandson of the original promoter had booked a long weekend of performances to celebrate the fiftieth anniversary of the last show. Some veteran performers would be there, along with a number of up-and-coming acts. Anticipation ran high in town at the prospect of an influx of tourists and musical artists.

"Jacob has been digging into bluegrass culture, hoping to create some signature dishes. I think he and Marshall are cooking up something together," Hannah said as she sipped from her own cup, which was not decaf. She needed the energy for her busy day. Jacob Forrest—head chef at Hannah's restaurant, the Hot Spot—was known for his creativity, and local food critic Marshall Fredericks often spurred him on.

"I'm glad Marshall's back." Liam smothered a yawn.

"You and Raquel both. She's been humming bluegrass tunes as she serves our patrons." Hannah glanced at the clock on the wall. "Speaking of bluegrass, I need to head over to the library in about ten minutes. Evangeline Cooke asked us to be there by nine to begin setting up an exhibit."

"For the festival?"

"Yes. Eddie Conley's wife, Beverly, is friends with Evangeline and Phyllis Taft of the historical society. Beverly told them there was a shack full of memorabilia from the festival out at their farm. Phyllis originally planned a small display, but there were so many crates and containers that they decided to do a special commemorative display in the main library instead."

"Eddie was part of the original duo, right?"

Hannah laughed as she set down her mug. "Bonus points for the boyfriend. Eddie was the mandolin player."

"Fiancé," Liam corrected. "Soon-to-be husband." He reached across the table and took Hannah's hand in his. "I can't wait to marry you, but I love that we have mornings like this—just the two of us together with no talk of wedding plans."

Hannah basked in his gentle smile. "Thank you for suggesting the break. I'm keeping a list of the things we need to make decisions on—guests, venue, catering, flowers, and of course a dress." She stopped and took a breath. "It's a little overwhelming, but we have time. For now, I want to enjoy being together, cherishing everything I love about you."

"I love you too." The words slid off his lips so easily that it was hard to believe there had ever been a time she'd been unsure of his affection.

"Are you planning to come to the Hot Spot for dinner tonight?" Hannah asked.

"Missing me already?"

Hannah laughed. "Guilty as charged."

"Why don't I come with you to see if Evangeline and Phyllis need more help?"

"I thought you needed sleep," Hannah reminded him.

"After being out on the festival grounds last night and now hearing about the memorabilia shed, I'm intrigued. It reminds me of our visit to the Bluegrass Hall of Fame when we were searching for your great-uncle Chuck last fall. Besides, I'm feeling more energized now. Your smile gives me more of a kick start than Zane's coffee."

Hannah smiled as she shook her head. "No surprise when you're drinking decaf."

Liam waved away her protest. "Decaf has no effect on my love for your smile. So, should I come help?"

Hannah agreed, happy to have his company for a little longer. Once they'd finished their refreshments, they waved goodbye to Zane and headed over to the library. It was a short and pleasant journey as they strolled hand in hand, greeting friends they met along the way.

They were halfway up the library steps when a voice caught Hannah's attention. "Hannah Prentiss?"

Hannah looked around to see who was calling her name. When she saw a stylish young woman with wavy strawberry-blond hair dressed in a denim skirt and cowboy boots hurrying toward the steps, a broad smile broke across her face. "Monroe Taylor? Is that you? I haven't seen you since our first high school reunion. Well, except on television. I hear you're taking the country music world by storm."

Monroe ducked her head in the demure way Hannah remembered. It was funny to think of her performing in front of thousands of fans. She'd always been so shy in school.

"Are you here for the festival?" Hannah asked. "Please tell me you're performing."

"I am. I'll do some sets with my mom and then some of my own with my band."

Liam still stood by the door, so Hannah made introductions. "Liam, this is Monroe Taylor. We were friends all the way back in kindergarten. She's the granddaughter of Eddie Conley, who we were talking about earlier. Monroe, meet Liam Berthold, Blackberry Valley's fire chief and my fiancé."

"A pleasure to meet you, Monroe." Liam inclined his head as he greeted her. He'd been two years ahead of them in school, so he and Hannah had run in different circles.

"And you too, Liam. Congratulations!" she exclaimed as she embraced Hannah. Then she studied Liam. "I think I remember your father. Didn't he used to do visits to the elementary school? Stop, drop, and roll."

"That's right. I'm glad you remember what he taught you." Liam held the door open for them.

They stepped into the main room of the library, which currently bore no resemblance to the quiet sanctuary of books and readers Hannah had come to expect. Pandemonium reigned. Boxes were stacked against the wall, and crates overflowing with instruments and posters formed a line down the middle of the room. Evangeline, looking somewhat flustered, ushered a few crying children and their harried mothers into the children's section. She collared one of the young volunteers to read a story. When she turned back toward the main room, Hannah caught a look of resignation on her face.

In the middle of the chaos stood the seventy-eight-year-old director of the historical center, Phyllis Taft, cool as a cucumber, directing volunteers as they unpacked the boxes.

Evangeline approached Hannah. "I'm so glad to see you. And Liam, you are a blessing. There are some bigger crates that need moving." She rolled her eyes at Monroe. "When your grandmother told me she had memorabilia, I never expected all this." Evangeline took a deep breath and slowly released it as Hannah patted her shoulder. "I'm trying to stay positive, and one thing is certain—we are going to give Blackberry Valley an exhibit to remember."

"What can we do to help?" Monroe asked.

"I'm deferring to Phyllis on this," Evangeline replied. "As director of the historical center, she's technically in charge. You might be able to help organize, though. Do you know anything about what's in these crates?"

Monroe shook her head sadly. "As far as I know, it was all stored away fifty years ago and hasn't been touched since. I can't even imagine the condition some of it must be in."

"It won't be that bad," Evangeline assured her. "Your grand-mother told me she had some storage company go through it in the early eighties. It was clear there would be no more festivals, but she didn't have the heart to get rid of everything. The workers put things into the proper protective cases." She grimaced. "It's a shame, but I just don't know where we're going to find places to display all of this."

"I have an idea," Hannah said. "With your grandparents' per-mission, Monroe, we could display some of the posters at the Hot Spot. My dad might even be able to make up another display case for some of the smaller, less valuable items."

"The Hot Spot?" Monroe gave her a questioning look.

"It's the farm-to-table restaurant I own here in town. Your grandmother sometimes joins Evangeline and other friends there for dinner."

"Hannah converted the old firehouse," Evangeline explained.

"Really? That sounds amazing."

"Amazing is exactly the word to describe the food her chef turns out," Liam said. "I highly recommend the—"

Hannah cut him off. "Don't trust any of his recommendations unless you have a high tolerance for spice. But you will have to come by and visit. Liam's right. My chef, Jacob Forrest, is a whiz in the kitchen, and he's working on some specials for the festival."

"Oh, that sounds tempting."

"Hey, Hannah." Lacy waved from across the room where she and her mother, Christine, were going through a box of news clippings.

"Lacy Johnston?"

"Monroe? How lovely to see you. And it's Lacy Minyard now." Lacy pushed away from the table and stood, smoothing her light maternity dress before she eased through the maze of boxes toward them. She hugged her girlhood friend as best she could with her belly between them. "It is so good to see you."

"And you. Look at you! When is the baby due?"

Lacy beamed. "Very soon. Well, actually, it just feels that way. I still have two months to go. You're in town for the festival, right? Are you performing?"

Monroe repeated the explanation she'd given Hannah.

"That sounds like so much fun," Lacy gushed. "What about your granddad? Is he going to make an appearance? You know the question on everyone's mind is whether we'll see a reunion of the Blackberry Mountain Boys."

Monroe's face fell, and she shook her head. "I'm sorry people will be disappointed, but he won't appear. He hasn't performed much since the last night of the festival in '76, the night his mandolin was stolen along with all the proceeds from the weekend. From what I've been told, it was as if the light went out of him. The band broke up that night, and Nana says he hasn't been the same since."

Hannah grimaced. "I can't even imagine. But don't worry about letting people down. We'll have lots of other great acts, including Monroe Taylor."

Monroe shot Hannah a grateful smile. "Okay, let's see what we can do to help Mrs. Taft make something special out of all of this."

"Oh, Monroe." Phyllis welcomed her with a one-armed hug as she juggled a clipboard and pen in her other hand. "You're just the person I've been waiting for. I need someone to help sort through this crate of instruments. I was thinking we could make an informational display showcasing the types of instruments traditionally played in a bluegrass band. Hannah, I was thinking of what you've done with the fire department memorabilia at the Hot Spot. I was going to use the photos here, but then this crate of instruments showed up, and that'll be so interesting visually." She gestured to the open crate sitting in a corner.

"We can do that, right, Monroe?"

"Sure. I lean more toward country, but I grew up surrounded by bluegrass, so I definitely know all the instruments." They headed for the corner and got right to work.

"What do you think about pulling everything out and spreading it on this study table so we can see what we've got?" Hannah suggested.

"Sounds good to me. What was Phyllis talking about that you did at your restaurant?"

Hannah reached into the crate to lift out a battered old banjo case. "About a year ago, shortly after I opened the Hot Spot, we got a rather savage review from the local restaurant critic. It was a good learning experience for us. One of the things he criticized was that 'the theming felt generic, like one might find in a chain restaurant anywhere in America.'" Hannah used her fingers to make air quotes. "And yes, I memorized every critical word so I knew what to fix. We all worked hard to do better, and now we're a success."

"So how did you update the theme?"

Hannah grinned. "Liam, his grandfather, and my dad took care of that. Liam's grandfather used to be fire chief. He sent Liam with a box of old photos and newspaper clippings and even his grandmother's diary. My dad made a display case. Marshall Fredericks—he's the food critic—was right in his critique. If you're going to convert the old firehouse into a restaurant and theme your menu accordingly, then the decor should reflect it. And now it does, as you'll see when you visit."

"Can't wait." Monroe lifted a case from the crate and handed it to Hannah, who opened it and set the guitar on the table. "I wonder why all these instruments are in here. I'll have to ask my grandparents. Maybe they were backups for the band members, but then why didn't those members keep them?"

"What's that?" Hannah asked when Monroe opened up the next case. It was some kind of guitar with a fancy metal front that looked like a hubcap.

"That's a Dobro. It's an acoustic guitar with a resonator that gives bluegrass its distinctive metallic sound. We use it in country music too."

"Is that everything?" Hannah asked as she set the Dobro on the table. There was no reply. When she glanced back, Monroe was staring intently at the instrument she was holding. "Is something wrong?"

Monroe sank onto a stool and cradled the instrument in her arms as she glanced up. Her voice shook as she spoke. "Hannah, this is Grandpa Eddie's missing mandolin."

Hannah gaped. "But how? I mean I thought it was stolen."

"It was. But I'm holding it in my hands right now."

"Are you sure?"

Monroe nodded slowly. "Without a doubt. I grew up surrounded by photos of Grandpa playing this mandolin. I used to study the images, trying to understand what was so special about it. See this little mark here?" She pointed to a slight indentation on the scroll.

"Apparently, Grandpa Eddie had a tendency to rub it when he was getting ready to play. He wore it down with his thumb over the years. And this little scratch?" She laughed. "Nana said her kitten was trying to play with it and wasn't happy when Grandpa took it away."

Hannah chuckled at the mental image.

Monroe's fingers reverently stroked the maple neck, but she suddenly jerked them away as if she'd been burned. She lowered her head and closely examined the mandolin. Her voice sounded confused when she continued. "This was not the way it looked in the photos. This instrument has been broken and glued back together."

"What?"

"Look."

Hannah knelt beside her and examined the section Monroe pointed to. "That *is* glued, and they didn't even do a good job." She peered up at her friend. "What do we do now?"

Monroe blew out a breath. "I don't know. I want to take it to Grandpa Eddie, but I guess we should call the sheriff first. He'll know what to do."

Hannah nodded. "That's a good idea. Besides, I have some questions. Where did this mandolin come from? Who put it in this crate? Was it the person who stole it?" She paused as a thought occurred to her. "Didn't you say the mandolin and money were stolen together?"

Monroe's eyes grew wider as she followed Hannah's line of thinking. "If the mandolin and money were stolen together, where is the money?"

Loved *Mysteries of Blackberry Valley?*
Check out some other Guideposts mystery series!

Whistle Stop Café Mysteries

Join best friends Debbie Albright and Janet Shaw as they step out in faith to open the Whistle Stop Café inside the historic train depot in Dennison, Ohio. During WWII, the depot's canteen workers offered doughnuts, sandwiches, and a heap of gratitude to thousands of soldiers on their way to war via troop-transport trains. Our sleuths soon find themselves on track to solve baffling mysteries—both past and present. Come along for the ride for stories of honor, duty to God and country, and of course fun, family, and friends!

Under the Apple Tree
As Time Goes By
We'll Meet Again
Till Then
I'll Be Seeing You
Fools Rush In
Let It Snow
Accentuate the Positive
For Sentimental Reasons

That's My Baby
A String of Pearls
Somewhere Over the Rainbow
Down Forget-Me-Not Lane
Set the World on Fire
When You Wish Upon a Star
Rumors Are Flying
Here We Go Again
Stairway to the Stars
Winter Weather
Wait Till the Sun Shines
Now You're in My Arms
Sooner or Later
Apple Blossom Time
My Dreams Are Getting Better

Secrets from Grandma's Attic

Life is recorded not only in decades or years, but in events and memories that form the fabric of our being. Follow Tracy Doyle, Amy Allen, and Robin Davisson, the granddaughters of the recently deceased centenarian, Pearl Allen, as they explore the treasures found in the attic of Grandma Pearl's Victorian home, nestled near the banks of the Mississippi in Canton, Missouri. Not only do Pearl's descendants uncover a long-buried mystery at every attic exploration, they also discover their grandmother's legacy of deep, abiding faith, which has shaped and guided their family through the years. These uncovered Secrets from Grandma's Attic reveal stories of faith, redemption, and second chances that capture your heart long after you turn the last page.

Savannah Secrets

Welcome to Savannah, Georgia, a picture-perfect Southern city known for its manicured parks, moss-covered oaks, and antebellum architecture. Walk down one of the cobblestone streets, and you'll come upon Magnolia Investigations. It is here where two friends have joined forces to unravel some of Savannah's deepest secrets. Tag along as clues are exposed, red herrings discarded, and thrilling surprises revealed. Find inspiration in the special bond between Meredith Bellefontaine and Julia Foley. Cheer the friends on as they listen to their hearts and rely on their faith to solve each new case that comes their way.

The Waving Girl
Beneath a Dragon Moon
Garden Variety Crimes
Meant for Good
A Bone to Pick
Honeybees & Legacies
True Grits
Sapphire Secret
Jingle Bell Heist
Buried Secrets
A Puzzle of Pearls
Facing the Facts
Resurrecting Trouble
Forever and a Day

Mysteries of Martha's Vineyard

Priscilla Latham Grant has inherited a lighthouse! So with not much more than a strong will and a sore heart, the recent widow says goodbye to her lifelong Kansas home and heads to the quaint and historic island of Martha's Vineyard, Massachusetts. There, she comes face-to-face with adventures, which include her trusty canine friend, Jake, three delightful cousins she didn't know she had, and Gerald O'Bannon, a handsome Coast Guard captain—plus head-scratching mysteries that crop up with surprising regularity.

A Light in the Darkness
Like a Fish Out of Water
Adrift
Maiden of the Mist
Making Waves
Don't Rock the Boat
A Port in the Storm
Thicker Than Water
Swept Away
Bridge Over Troubled Waters
Smoke on the Water
Shifting Sands
Shark Bait

Seascape in Shadows
Storm Tide
Water Flows Uphill
Catch of the Day
Beyond the Sea
Wider Than an Ocean
Sheeps Passing in the Night
Sail Away Home
Waves of Doubt
Lifeline
Flotsam & Jetsam
Just Over the Horizon

A Note from the Editors

We hope you enjoyed another exciting volume in the Mysteries of Blackberry Valley series, published by Guideposts. For over seventy-five years, Guideposts, a nonprofit organization, has been driven by a vision of a world filled with hope. We aspire to be the voice of a trusted friend, a friend who makes you feel more hopeful and connected.

By making a purchase from Guideposts, you join our community in touching millions of lives, inspiring them to believe that all things are possible through faith, hope, and prayer. Your continued support allows us to provide uplifting resources to those in need. Whether through our communities, websites, apps, or publications, we inspire our audiences, bring them together, and comfort, uplift, entertain, and guide them. Visit us at guideposts.org to learn more.

We would love to hear from you. Write us at Guideposts, P.O. Box 5815, Harlan, Iowa 51593 or call us at (800) 932-2145. Did you love *A Brush with Danger*? Leave a review for this product on guideposts.org/shop. Your feedback helps others in our community find relevant products.

Find inspiration, find faith, find Guideposts.
Shop our best sellers and favorites at
guideposts.org/shop
Or scan the QR code to go directly to our Shop

More Great Mysteries
Are Waiting For Readers Like *You!*

Whistle Stop Café Mysteries

*"Memories of a lifetime...I loved reading this story.
Could not put the book down...."* —ROSE H.

Mystery and WWII historical fiction fans will love these intriguing novels where two close friends piece together clues to solve mysteries past and present. Set in the real town of Dennison, Ohio, at a historic train depot where many soldiers once set off for war, these stories are filled with faithful, relatable characters you'll love spending time with.

Mysteries & Wonders of the Bible

*"I so enjoyed this book....What a great insight into the life of
the women who wove the veil for the Temple."* —SHIRLEYN J.

Have you ever wondered what it might have been like to live back in Bible times to experience miraculous Bible events firsthand? Then you'll LOVE the fascinating **Mysteries & Wonders of the Bible** novels! Each Scripture-inspired story whisks you back to the ancient Holy Land, where you'll accompany ordinary men and women in their search for the hidden truths behind some of the most pivotal moments in the Bible. Each volume includes insights from a respected biblical scholar to help you ponder the significance of each story to your own life.

Mysteries of Cobble Hill Farm

*"Wonderful series. Great story. Spellbinding. Could not put
it down once I started reading."* —BONNIE C.

Escape to the charming English countryside with **Mysteries of Cobble Hill Farm**, a heartwarming series of faith-filled mysteries. Harriet Bailey relocates to Yorkshire, England, to take over her late grandfather's veterinary practice, hoping it's the fresh start she needs. As she builds a new life, Harriet uncovers modern mysteries and long-buried secrets in the village and among the rolling hills and castle ruins. Each book is an inspiring puzzle where God's gentlest messengers—the animals in her care—help Harriet save the day.

Learn More & Shop These Exciting Mysteries, Biblical Stories, & Other Uplifting Fiction at **guideposts.org/fiction**